ALL YOU HAVE TO DO IS ASK . . .

Why are bad dreams called nightmares?

Why, when we wish an actor good luck, do we say "break a leg?"

Why did women start wearing high heels?

Why is there an eye at the top of the pyramid on the dollar bill?

Why, when Yankee Doodle put a feather in his cap, did he call it macaroni?

Why is ice cream served in cones?

Why is the United States personified by Uncle Sam?

MORE EVER WONDER WHY?

Douglas B. Smith

FAWCETT GOLD MEDAL • NEW YORK

A Fawcett Gold Medal Book
Published by Ballantine Books
Copyright © 1994 by Douglas B. Smith

Library of Congress Catalog Card Number: 93-90869

ISBN 0-449-14887-4

Manufactured in the United States of America

First Edition: April 1994

10   9   8   7   6   5   4   3   2   1

To Jeannette and David

Preface

More Ever Wonder Why, like its predecessor *Ever Wonder Why*, provides the reader with plausible explanations of some of the peculiar things we see about us. In most cases, we can figure out the reasons behind the things we see, say, or do, but in some cases, the reasons are not so obvious, like why so many taxicabs are yellow, why computer errors are called "bugs," and why we wish an actor good luck by telling him to "break a leg." This book is about the "not-so-obvious" things.

The explanations are described as plausible, because in most cases, more than one explanation can be found. Authorities frequently disagree—sometimes vehemently—and there is usually no way to determine with absolute certainty which authority is correct. The answers given in this book are those about which most authorities seem to agree or, in the absence of such agreement, those that seem the most reasonable to the author.

The research that went into this book provided the author with many months of enjoyment. It is hoped that the book will provide the reader with a couple of hours of entertainment.

Acknowledgments

The author wishes to thank the following people who provided valuable assistance in researching, verifying, and editing the material in this book: Dr. O. F. Schuette, Rudy Mancke, George Fowler, Brent Smith, Lottie McMahon, Hazel Poston, A. Harrison McLaurin, Bob Stein, Jack Lovelady, Charles Poole, and the excellent research librarians at the South Carolina State Library. Thanks also to James Ellisor, who did an excellent job of preparing the manuscript, and to Knox Burger and Elisa Wares, who provided their usual fine support.

Ever Wonder Why?

—a section of town containing houses of prostitution is called a "red-light district"?

In the early days of the railroad, it was customary for railroad men to hang a red oil lamp on the last car of a train to keep other trains from running into it from the rear. It was also customary for these men to carry the oil lamps into town to have them refilled when the train made a stop. Quite frequently, the bearers of the red lamps were known to make stops at local houses of prostitution on their way to or from town, and when they did, they usually left their red lamp hanging on the front porch. It was the sight of these red lamps that gave us the expression "red-light district." The name caught on, and brothel owners began identifying their establishments by putting permanent red lights on their porches.

—grass in Kentucky is blue?

When Kentucky bluegrass (Poa pratensis) blooms around the middle of June, the color of its seed vessels gives the landscape a bluish tint.

Ever Wonder Why?

—Chinese women used to bind their feet?
This practice began as a fashion trend but later became a means of keeping women in the home.

Chinese court dancers used to bind their feet just enough to give them a crescent shape. The dancers would then perform on their toes, in ballerina style, dancing and twirling in the centers of carved lotus flowers. Ladies of the Chinese upper-class liked the looks of these crescent-shaped feet and began binding their own feet in a similar fashion.

Around the twelfth century, a time when new concepts of female chastity were developing in China, it became a symbol of status for a man's wife to remain at home and not be seen in the fields or on the streets. To ensure that their wives would remain at home, Chinese men began binding their wives' feet so tightly that it deformed the foot and made prolonged walking too painful to endure.

Ever Wonder Why?

—the scale in music is sung, "do re mi fa so la ti do"?

This particular scale was devised by an Italian singing teacher named Guido d'Arezzo. For his notes he used the first syllable of the first six lines of a Latin hymn to St. John. The first six lines were:

Ut queant laxis
*Re*sonare fibris
*Mi*ra gestorum
*Fa*muli tuorum
*Sol*ve polluti
*La*bii reatum Sancte Joannes.

The scale, therefore, was originally "ut re mi fa sol la."

"Ut" was changed to "do" to make the scales more singable, and the syllables "ti" and "do" were later added at the end to make an octave.

—the Hatfields and the McCoys feuded for 17 years?

The Hatfields of West Virginia and the McCoys of Kentucky lived on opposite sides of a small stream on the Kentucky-West Virginia border, and although they were on different sides during the Civil War, there was no fighting between them until 1873. That was when Randolph McCoy accused Floyd Hatfield of stealing a hog. A very tense trial was held, and family members on both sides showed up armed. The jury deadlocked, and the shooting began. There was much bloodshed on both sides, and things didn't cool down until 1890. Thirty years later, the two clans were intermarrying.

Ever Wonder Why?

—NBC plays those three musical notes with its logo on TV?

On the musical scale, those notes are G-E-C, and they represent the General Electric Corporation, the company that owns NBC.

—most Latins have dark eyes?

In the hotter climates where Latins live, inhabitants are exposed to more sunlight during the year than in regions further north or south. To adapt to this intense radiation, the eyes of natives have, over the centuries, developed extra amounts of pigment, causing their eyes to appear dark. Such additional protective pigment also accounts for their dark hair and skin.

—the Grim Reaper carries a scythe?

Many of our ancestors greatly feared the dead and firmly believed that, unless stopped, the dead would rise out of their graves at night and roam the countryside terrorizing the living. These ghostly rampages could be prevented, they believed, by burying sharp instruments with the dead bodies, the presumption being that the deceased beings would be afraid to make a move for fear of being cut. It, therefore, became common practice in countries like Hungary and Romania to bury a sickle or scythe with the dead. When such graves were later excavated, they were found to contain a skeleton, a shroud, and a scythe, and it was this image of death, we assume, that led to our current depiction of the Grim Reaper.

Ever Wonder Why?

—a cheap cigar is called a "stogie"?

Drivers of the big Conestoga wagons of the past spent most of their days on the road and most of their nights sleeping under harsh conditions in wagon houses along their route. Knowing that these low-paid but dedicated drivers were avid smokers, a cigar manufacturer decided to make a special cigar just for them. The cigars were large, made with low-grade tobacco, and so cheap that they weren't given an official name. The drivers began calling the cigars "Conestogas," then "Conestogies," and finally, just "stogies."

—some people kiss the tips of their fingers, then toss their hand forward to show praise?

In certain religious cultures, it was once customary to express love for a deity by kissing a sacred object. At times, however, worshipers weren't allowed to get close enough to a sacred object to kiss it. So, they devised a way to kiss the object from a distance. They placed a kiss on their fingertips and then tossed their fingers in the direction of the worshiped object. This is why we sometimes show love or praise by kissing our fingertips and tossing our hand forward.

Ever Wonder Why?

—so many churches have stained-glass windows?

The use of stained glass grew out of the art of mosaics, which involves the mounting of small pieces of cut stone in plaster as a form of decoration. Mosaics, it is believed, originated in ancient Crete where beach pebbles were first imbedded in cement to make decorative flooring. By the 4th century B.C., mosaics had taken pictorial form and were used to depict mythical figures. Later, pieces of pigmented glass were added to designs, and mosaics began to appear on walls, especially in places of worship, where they were used to illustrate religious scenes and stories. Eventually it was realized that the effect of colored glass mosaics could be made more dramatic by arranging the mosaics so that light passed through them. To achieve this effect, the pieces of cut glass were mounted between metal strips and the resulting mosaics placed in window openings, giving us stained-glass windows. They have remained a popular feature of churches ever since.

—crude iron direct from a blast furnace is called "pig" iron?

When molten iron leaves a blast furnace, it is poured into a series of sand molds to cool. These molds are connected at right angles to a feeder channel, and when full of molten iron, they resemble suckling pigs nursing a sow. Hence, the name "pig" iron.

Ever Wonder Why?

—fireflies flash?

Since fireflies are active at night, they need some way to find members of the opposite sex in the dark. The flashing of their abdomens provides this.

The male firefly makes a courtship flight a few feet above the ground, flashing its abdomen in a pattern unique to its species. The female watches from the ground, and when she spots the right pattern, she begins to flash her own abdomen. The male sees this, flies to the female, and they mate.

The phosphorescent light is due to a chemical reaction triggered by a nerve impulse.

—an extremely happy person is said to be in "seventh heaven"?

The Muslims believe that there are seven levels of heaven, with each level offering a greater degree of bliss than the one below it. The seventh heaven is at the highest level and, therefore, the one offering the greatest degree of happiness. Anyone in the seventh heaven, then, is said to be in a state of supreme joy.

Ever Wonder Why?

—most roadside mailboxes are of the exact same size, shape, and design?

Around the turn of the century, almost every imaginable container was used as a mail receptacle on rural delivery routes; there were baskets, orange crates, oil cans, cigar boxes, lard pails, old tires—and even cracks in fence posts. This became quite a problem for mail carriers who had to get down from their buggies at each stop, walk over to the makeshift container, and deposit the mail in a receptacle that may or may not protect the mail from the elements. To correct this problem, Congress authorized the Postmaster General in 1902 to adopt a standard mailbox that would meet certain minimum requirements as to size, height, durability, accessibility, and security. Many designs were considered, but none was settled upon until 1915. At that time, a post office employee named Roy J. Joroleman designed the current tunnel-shaped metal box with the pull-down door and metal flag. The Postmaster General endorsed the design and authorized manufacturers who produced such boxes to mark them "Approved by the Postmaster General." Thus began the production of the millions of identical mailboxes we see today.

—some bridges are covered?

Covers were put on bridges to protect the wooden components of the bridge from the weather. This was believed to be cheaper in the long run than periodically replacing rotted structural members.

Ever Wonder Why?

—corporate stock inflated beyond its real value is called "watered" stock?

We owe this expression to Daniel Drew who, prior to becoming a notorious stock manipulator in the robber baron era, was in the cattle business. It is said that before Drew brought his cattle to market, he would deprive them of water and feed them salt to make them thirsty. Then, on the day before the sale, he would allow the cattle to gulp down as much water as they could hold. The extra water would increase the cow's weight beyond what it would have normally been, thereby allowing Drew to charge a higher price for his "watered" stock.

When Drew went into the brokerage business, he employed a similar deception by selling additional shares of stock in corporations he controlled without adding anything to the corporation's assets. Thus, the value of the corporate stock was inflated in much the same way as had been the livestock, and this led people to describe such stock as "watered."

—when two people walk on opposite sides of an obstacle, one of them says "bread and butter"?

This practice is based on an old superstition that says if a physical object comes between two friends while they are walking together, it could be an omen that their friendship is near an end. According to the superstition, the effect of the omen can be reversed if one of the friends will say, out loud, the name of two items normally joined together. Hence the practice of saying "bread and butter."

Ever Wonder Why?

—bruises turn black and blue?

A bruise is caused by a blow that is hard enough to break the tiny blood vessels under the skin. This causes blood to seep into surrounding areas where it can no longer get the oxygen that was supplied through the blood vessels. Since it is oxygen that gives blood its red color, this oxygen-deprived blood now turns blue. Any part of this blue blood that is seen through pink or reddened skin will appear black, thus giving bruises their black and blue appearance.

—errors in computers are called "bugs"?

One of the earliest computer bugs was, in fact, a real bug. An error in one of the first digital computers, the Mark I, was traced to a moth that had died in one of the computer's relays. This prompted Grace Hopper—one of the programmers working on the Mark I and a very notable computer pioneer—to begin calling all computer errors "bugs." Correcting the errors soon became known as "debugging."

—Intercourse, Pennsylvania, has that name?

The town bearing this name was once the home of a racecourse. To provide directions to the course, the townspeople erected a sign at the edge of town marking the course's entrance. It read "ENTER COURSE." It was a corruption of the spelling of this sign that led to the town being called, and finally named Intercourse, Pennsylvania.

Ever Wonder Why?

—the American eagle is called a "bald" eagle?

When the eagle was given this name, the word "bald" meant "white" rather than hairless. Originally the bird was called a bald-headed eagle, meaning white-headed eagle. In the late 1700s the name was shortened to bald eagle.

—Venus de Milo has no arms?

As originally sculpted in the 2nd century B.C., the statue had arms, but by the time it was rediscovered on the Island of Melos in 1820, the arms had been broken off and lost. Some say that the lady of the statue originally held a shield and was looking at her reflection in it. The tip of the nose was also broken off but was replaced.

—an informer is called a "stool pigeon"?

Pigeon meat was considered a rare delicacy around the mid-nineteenth century, and a captured pigeon was much preferred to one that had been shot, since the shooting of a pigeon usually damaged the meat. Hunters, therefore, set about to devise ways to capture live pigeons, and one of these involved using another pigeon as a decoy.

The decoy pigeon was usually tied with a long string to the leg of a stool on which the hunter sat—sometimes for hours—waiting for a wild pigeon to come within range. The decoy bird used to lure others into captivity became known as a stool pigeon, a term that now describes someone who causes another to be captured.

Ever Wonder Why?

—bells are put on cows?

If a cow is hungry or painfully full of milk, she will voluntarily come back to the barn. But if this isn't the case, the cow may not come back on her own, meaning that the farmer must go find her. Since finding a cow in a large pasture full of trees and rolling hills can be very difficult, farmers began tying clanging bells around the necks of their cows to make the job easier.

—a coward is said to be "lily-livered"?

To the ancient Greeks, the liver was thought to be the center of emotion in a person. A person with a dark liver, one containing much bile, was thought to be strong and passionate, while a man with a deficiency of bile, or a lily-white liver, was believed to be weak or cowardly.

—pistachios are red?

The natural color of the pistachio shell is not red but pale yellow or yellow-green. Suppliers of the nuts began dying them to hide harmless but unsightly blemishes and stains that are usually found on the shells. Many colors were used originally, but red proved to be the most popular, and the other colors were discontinued.

—we say someone is mad as a March hare?

Spring is the mating season for hares, and during March, the male hares often jump about, fight savagely with other male hares, and exhibit seemingly insane behavior. This may account for the expression.

Ever Wonder Why?

—flamingos are pink?

Flamingos feed on algae and crustaceans such as shrimp that contain the red pigment carotenoid. It is this pigment that gives the flamingos' feathers their pink color. When flamingos in captivity are deprived of the carotenoid pigment, the pink color disappears, leaving a white bird.

—women started wearing high heels?

The trend toward high heels began in France during the 16th century, and it was men, not women, who originated the custom. Men found that the higher heels enabled them to get better foothold on their stirrups and also raised their feet a few inches above the filth found in the streets at that time.

Women didn't take up the custom until the reign of Louis XIV. King Louis was a rather short man who had his cobblers add several inches to his heels to make him appear taller. Copying this royal trend, both men and women began wearing higher heels—sometimes as much as three inches higher. After the end of Louis's reign, the men returned to their normal-sized heels, but the women—apparently enjoying their taller stature—did not. They continued to wear high, but much narrower, heels. By the 18th century, American women took the fashion lead from France and also began wearing "French heels."

Ever Wonder Why?

—hospital administrators insist that discharged patients leave the hospital in wheelchairs?

Until a patient is off of the hospital grounds, the hospital is legally liable for anything that happens to him or her. Since many patients leaving a hospital are still a bit weak or, perhaps, still feeling the effects of anesthesia, hospital administrators have decided to take precautions to make sure that patients don't fall and injure themselves on the hospital's premises. Therefore, they ask all discharged patients to ride out of the hospital in a wheelchair.

—the first automobiles looked so odd?

They looked that way because they were designed to look like horse buggies. This is why they had high seats, no tops, and no windshields. The first automobiles were, in fact, called horseless carriages and the first garages, automobile stables.

—a man in women's clothes is said to be "in drag"?

This expression comes from the early theater when men often had to play women's roles. Since the dresses they wore "dragged" when the actor walked across the stage, these roles were known as drag roles, and the actors playing them were said to be "in drag."

—a whip cracks?

Part of the sound you hear is due to the slap of the tip of the whip as it snaps back upon itself, but the loudest part of the sound is a sonic boom. When the tip reverses its direction and circles back, it is traveling so fast that it actually breaks the sound barrier.

Ever Wonder Why?

—vagrants are called "hobos"?

After the Civil War, migratory farm workers frequently rode the rails looking for work. Since much of the work they did was done with a hoe, most of the workers carried their own hoes. As a result, the workers became known as "hoe boys," a term that was later abbreviated to "hobos." By 1891, the term had come to mean any vagrant.

—a spider doesn't get caught in its own web?

Two things prevent a spider from getting caught in its web.

Spiderwebs consist of spirals of sticky threads arranged on a framework of dry, slippery threads that radiate out from the center. The spider simply walks on the dry threads, thereby avoiding the sticky substance. It keeps from slipping by grasping the slippery strands with curved claws extending from its legs.

It is not certain, however, that even the most agile of spiders won't one day slide into the gummy threads, so, nature has coated the spider's legs with an oil that allows it to take short trips on the sticky substance without getting stuck.

—your side hurts when you run too hard?

The pain you feel is called a "stitch," and it occurs when a prolonged jolting motion—as would be experienced in running—puts an excessive stress on the ligaments that support the stomach, spleen, and liver. Bending over will often reduce the pain, because it removes some of the stress.

Ever Wonder Why?

—an unqualified doctor is called a "quack"?

"Quack" is an abbreviation of an old Dutch term "Quacksalver," meaning one who brags or boasts about his salves or ointments.

—stars twinkle and planets don't?

When we see a star, we are seeing a single point of light that has come to us from millions of miles away. As this tiny light passes through the earth's atmosphere, it is affected by air currents and turbulences that bend the light back and forth causing it to dim and brighten irregularly. This is what we see as a twinkle.

The reflected light from a planet, on the other hand, appears to us, not as a single point of light, but as a small disk composed of many points of light. This is because the planet is much nearer to us. As this bundle of points travels to earth, some of the points are affected by the earth's atmosphere just as starlight is, but since there are so many points of light in the disk, there are always enough nonaffected points to make the planet's light appear as a steady beam.

It is interesting to note that stars appear to twinkle less on calm nights or when they are viewed from high in the mountains. This is because, in the first case, there is less air turbulence to disturb the star's light and, in the second case, there is less atmosphere through which the star's light must travel. When there is no atmosphere at all between the viewer and the stars, the stars do not twinkle but are seen as unwavering points of light. This is how stars appear to astronauts in space.

Ever Wonder Why?

—we say something is "selling like hotcakes"?
Hotcakes cooked in grease or lard and served piping hot were a very popular item at county fairs, carnivals, and church bazaars around the turn of the century. These hotcakes always sold as fast as they could be made, and this led to the current expression "selling like hotcakes."

—the White Cliffs of Dover are white?
These cliffs, which rise above the English Channel, are white because they are composed primarily of chalk. The chalk, which is a type of limestone, came from the shells and skeletons of small animals that lived in the waters that once covered the region where the cliffs now stand.

—the game of hopping in and out of squares drawn on the ground is called "hopscotch"?
"Scotch," in this case, means to cut or scratch. Since the pattern the players hop in and out of is scratched—or scotched—into the playing surface, the game was dubbed hopscotch.

Ever Wonder Why?

—gargoyles were put on buildings?

Originally, a gargoyle was just a stone waterspout extending from a gutter used to cause rainwater to fall away from the base of a building. During the 12th century, it became customary to carve gargoyles in the shape of grotesque beasts for reasons of superstition, the belief being that the horrible images would keep away evil spirits.

After lead drainpipes replaced stone waterspouts, it remained the custom to decorate buildings with the same type of carved figures, which continued to be referred to as gargoyles.

—we refer to jealousy as the "green-eyed monster"?

The "green-eyed monster" to which jealousy is being compared is most likely a cat, tiger, or some other member of the feline family. Such animals are noted for teasing and tormenting their victims before finally destroying them, and this has been compared to the way jealousy often affects its victims. In Othello, for instance, Shakespeare describes jealousy as "the green-eyed monster which doth mock the meat it feeds on."

Ever Wonder Why?

—S.O.S. soap pads are named that?

Around 1917, Edwin Cox, a door-to-door salesman in San Francisco was looking for a gimmick to increase his sales of cookware. Aware that cleaning pots and pans was a frequent problem for housewives, he developed a way to add soap to steel wool pads and began giving these as gifts to his customers. The soap pads were such a success that Cox soon went into the manufacture of them full time. As for the product's name, Cox's wife came up with the idea of using the international distress call S.O.S., saying that it stood for "Save Our Saucepans."

—people pull on a wishbone for good luck?

As early as 2,000 years ago, chickens in certain parts of the world were considered sacred and believed capable of imparting good luck. When a chicken was killed, its V-shaped collarbone was dried in the sun and put in a place where it could be stroked by believers. This custom, which originated with the Etruscans on the Italian Peninsula, was also observed much later by the Romans. Apparently, in Rome there weren't enough wishbones to meet the demand, because at some point, a struggle ensued when two persons grabbed for the same wishbone. When the bone broke, it was presumed that the good luck followed the larger piece, and this, it is suggested, gave rise to the custom of pulling on a wishbone for good luck.

Ever Wonder Why?

—listening in on another person's conversation is called "eavesdropping"?

Before gutters were a common fixture, most houses were built with large overhanging eaves designed to cause rainwater to fall away from the base of the house. The area under these eaves was called an eavesdrop, and anyone standing in this area to listen at a window was called an eavesdropper.

—the guitar is shaped the way it is?

It is widely agreed that the graceful curves of the guitar are meant to be suggestive of those of a woman.

—"hunky-dory" means satisfactory?

The expression may have come from Huncho-dori, a street in Yokohama, Japan. Huncho-dori was, in fact, the city's main street, and it was well-lit, well-policed, and considered safe for servicemen on shore leave. Other streets in Yokohama were not so safe, and anyone traveling them did so at their own peril. Therefore, when servicemen left their ships to go into Yokohama on shore leave, they were advised to confine their night's activities to Huncho-dori, which was usually pronounced "hunky-dory." So, if a serviceman said he was going to a "hunky-dory" establishment, that meant the place was on Huncho-dori street and, therefore, "okay," which may be why, today, we use the expression to mean satisfactory.

Ever Wonder Why?

—the phrase "Kilroy was here" was once so popular?

Kilroy was James J. Kilroy, a shipyard inspector from Quincy, Massachusetts, whose job it was to inspect crates, barrels, bundles, and packages about to be shipped to other ports. To indicate that he had inspected an item, he wrote "Kilroy was here" on the container. Containers bearing this phrase were shipped to all parts of the world, and this is how the phrase became popular.

—banks used to refuse checks written in red ink?

This was the practice in days when checks were microfilmed using orthochromatic film, which doesn't record the color red. Today, microfilming is done using panchromatic film which records all colors, and red ink is no longer a problem.

—some say it is very dangerous to wake a sleepwalker?

In many cultures, it was once believed that a person's soul was only loosely attached to his body and that it actually left the body during a deep sleep. It was further believed that if someone was awakened suddenly from such a deep sleep, it might prevent the soul from reentering the body and cause the person to die. Since a sleepwalker was thought to be in the deepest of sleeps, it was believed that to awaken him suddenly was to put his life in peril.

Ever Wonder Why?

—your nose runs when you cry?

A tube called the naso-lachrymal duct runs from a small hole in the inner corner of the eye to the nose, and when excess water builds up in the eye, this tube serves as a drainage system through the nose. Therefore, when you cry, some of the tears drain through the nose. Some of the tears also run out of the eyes because the naso-lachrymal duct is too small to handle a large volume of tears.

—a vampire does not cast a reflection in a mirror?

To our ancestors, a person's image in a pool of water or a mirror was often believed to be a reflection of that person's soul. Since, as everyone knows, vampires have no soul, they cast no reflection.

—the Tower of Pisa leans?

The eight-story tower was erected in 1174 on a sand foundation, and it began to lean after only three stories had been completed. The builders changed the design of the tower to compensate for the shift in weight and then completed the five remaining floors.

The tower continues to tilt more and more each year, and today it is about 17 feet out of alignment at the top. Some engineers predict that, eventually, the tower will tip over.

Ever Wonder Why?

—a grapefruit is called that when it bears no relation to a grape?

Early explorers in Barbados noticed that grapefruits grow in clusters like grapes and so gave them their name. Grapes themselves were named by the French after the *grape*, a small hook used to pull grapes off the vine.

—those popular snack cakes are called "Twinkies"?

They were named after a shoe! James Dewar, the man who invented the snack cake in 1930, saw a billboard advertising Twinkle-toe shoes. He noticed the similarity between the shoe and his little, oblong cake and decided to name his cakes "Twinkies."

—Christmas is sometimes written "Xmas"?

The "X" comes from the first letter of the Greek word for Christ, Xploto's.

—a horse race is sometimes called a Derby?

The Derby is named after Edward Stanley, the 12th Earl of Derby who, in 1780, established a special series of horse races for three-year olds.

—a bathroom on a ship is called a "head"?

Because bathrooms on ships were normally located in the bow, or head, of the ship.

Ever Wonder Why?

—the "BRIDGE ICES BEFORE ROAD"?

BRIDGE
ICES BEFORE
ROAD

In order for something to freeze, it must be able to give off its heat. When the temperature of the outside air drops, both a road and a bridge begin to give up their heat to the cold air. But the road, being in contact with the ground, is continually rewarmed by heat rising from below the earth's surface. The bridge being, for the most part, suspended in air, is not rewarmed in this manner and so freezes first.

—we say "sic 'em" to a dog?
This is simply a corrupted form of "seek him."

Ever Wonder Why?

—there is no "Q" or "Z" on a phone dial?

When phone numbers became longer and more difficult to remember, the phone company tried to help customers remember them by devising the 2/5 number plan—two letters followed by five digits. This meant that 265-2113 could be remembered as Amherst 5-2113, 287-5654 as Butterfield 7-5654, and so forth.

To implement the plan, letters were placed on the phone dial above each digit that might be used as the first digit of a phone number. Since the digit 1 was reserved for long-distance and the digit 0 for the operator, these digits could never be used as the first digit of a number, and so no letters were to be placed above them. This left 8 digits over which letters were to be placed. It had been decided earlier that, for purposes of symmetry, there would be the same number of letters over each digit. But this could not be done with 8 digits and 26 letters. So, the decision was made to drop 2 letters. Since the letters "Q" and "Z" were the least likely to appear as the first two letters of a word, they were the letters dropped.

Ever Wonder Why?

—Nero fiddled while Rome burned?

Nero did not fiddle in the usual sense of the word, since the fiddle, or violin, was not invented until 1500 years after Rome burned in 64 A.D. More likely, Nero played a small lute called a *fidicula*, in Latin. The similarity between "fidicula" and "fiddle," plus the fact that they are both stringed instruments, may account for the expression.

When the fire began, Nero was away from Rome in the town of Antium, and it is reported that when he learned about the fire, he hurried back to Rome to help extinguish it. When he arrived, though, the blaze was beyond control, and all Nero could do was watch it from afar, which it is said, he did from a rooftop. As he watched, he picked up his *fidicula*—not his fiddle—and played a song of sadness. However, some people who saw him do this reported later that he played gaily as the city burned, and he was eventually accused of actually starting the fire. His accusers said that he wanted to destroy Rome so he could rebuild it to his own liking.

—that lump in the front of the throat is called an "Adam's apple"?

According to an ancient folk tale, when Adam took a bite of the forbidden apple, a piece of it stuck in his throat, causing the bulge we now call the "Adam's apple." This bulge, which actually is a bit of the thyroid cartilage comprising the larynx, was supposedly then inherited by Adam's descendants as a reminder of man's original sin.

Ever Wonder Why?

—storks were chosen as the mythical deliverers of babies?

Storks were selected for this role probably because of their tendency to make their nests in chimneys. Seeing a stork perched atop a chimney provided parents with an easy way to answer the child's question, "Where do babies come from?"

—women of Africa's Ubangi tribe stretch their bottom lip?

There is a great deal of uncertainty about why the Ubangi women do this, but according to one explanation, it was done originally as a means of protection. It is told that, about a century ago, a Ubangi village was attacked by raiders who enslaved many of the Ubangi women, but who rejected one woman because she had a deformed lower lip. This supposedly gave the other Ubangi women the idea of protecting their young girls from future raiders by artificially deforming their lips. They chose to do this by slitting the lip and inserting successively larger disks into the slit as the girl grew.

—refusing to do business with someone is called "boycotting"?

Around 1880, a landlord's agent in Ireland got the worst of it when he tried to raise the rents of his tenants. The tenants joined together and not only refused to pay the higher rent but also refused to do any business or have any dealings whatsoever with the agent. As a result, the agent lost his position and had to leave town. The agent's name was Charles Boycott, and this type of retaliatory tactic henceforth became known as "boycotting."

Ever Wonder Why?

—leaves turn color in the fall?

During spring and summer, tree leaves contain three principle substances: xanthophyll which is yellow, carotene which is orange or red, and chlorophyll which is green. During the growing season chlorophyll is used in conjunction with the sunlight to produce the plant's food, and it is present in the leaf in such abundance that its color overshadows that of the xanthophyll and carotene. This is why we see the leaves as green during spring and summer.

In the fall, when the tree enters a dormant state, production of the chlorophyll ceases, and the chlorophyll that is present slowly decomposes. As this happens, the chlorophyll and its green color disappear, leaving, in varying amounts, the yellow xanthophyll and the red or orange carotene. This is what gives the leaf its yellow, red, or orange color in the fall.

—we say, "I'll be there with bells on"?

The horses that pulled certain wagons of the past often had attached to their collars a ring of six or seven bells, and it was the custom in those days for these bells to be given to anyone who helped repair the wagon when it broke down. Therefore, if one wished to say that his wagon would reach its destination quickly and without breaking down, he might say, "I'll be there with bells on!"

Ever Wonder Why?

—that big "HOLLYWOOD" sign was erected in the Hollywood hills?

The sign was erected in 1923 to identify a real estate development known as HOLLYWOODLAND. Around 1945, the last four letters fell down, leaving the now famous landmark.

—Popeye gets his strength from spinach?

This began as the result of a misplaced decimal point. At the time cartoonist Elzie Segar decided that his main character, Popeye, would get his strength from eating spinach, it was commonly believed that spinach contained extra high quantities of iron and that iron added to one's strength. In actuality, iron does not have any special effect on strength, and spinach does not contain unusually high quantities of it. The misconception arose because of an earlier study on the nutritional value of spinach that contained an error in the placement of a decimal point. The error made it appear that spinach contained 10 times more iron than it actually does.

Ever Wonder Why?

—someone spoiling for a fight is "on the warpath"?
The trails used by American Indian hunting parties were called hunting trails or paths, and the trails used by trading parties were called trading trails or paths. Similarly, the great routes between enemy Indian nations used by war parties were called warrior paths. Anyone on the warrior path was headed for a fight, and this accounts for our current expression. Over time, warrior path was shortened to "warpath."

—we say "For Pete's sake"?
This expression was originated by people who preferred not to use the name of Christ in the expression "For Christ's sake." Pete is Saint Peter.

—smooching is sometimes called "spooning"?
Two theories are given as to why the word "spooning" has this connotation. One holds that it is due to an old English custom according to which spoons delicately carved or engraved with lovers' hands were once exchanged between sweethearts. The other theory attributes the term to the way lovers look when they are lying together intimately—like spoons in a drawer.

Ever Wonder Why?

—an artist sights over his thumb when he looks at his subject?

This is done for two reasons. First, it enables the artist to estimate size relationships. For example, by comparing the width of his thumb to a table in the distance, he might find that the table is two thumbs high and four thumbs wide. Thus, he knows that, in his drawing, the table must be twice as wide as it is high.

Second, a thumb or pencil held vertically will reveal the approximate slant angles of objects being drawn.

Ever Wonder Why?

—bad dreams are called nightmares?

In some cultures, it was once believed that evil spirits called *mahrs* in Germany and *Mora* in Slavic countries came to people in the night and attacked them while they slept. These goblins would first frighten their victims with terrible dreams and then try to suffocate them. These night *mahrs* or night *Moras* gave rise to our term nightmares.

—pretzels are made in that loose-knot pattern?

Pretzels were invented by medieval monks who gave them as rewards to children for learning their prayers. The shape of the pretzel is supposed to represent a pair of arms folded across the child's chest in prayer.

—someone in a state of high agitation is described as being "beside himself"?

This saying came about at a time when it was believed that, under conditions of extreme stress, a person's soul might actually leave his body. If this happened, an agitated person might very well wind up "beside himself"—that is, standing beside his own soul.

Ever Wonder Why?

—a moth will circle a light at night?

Any explanation as to why an animal does what it does is, at best, a theory. The theory explaining this phenomena is as follows:

A moth manages to fly a straight line at night by keeping some distant light in a fixed position relative to its eye. For instance, the moth might keep the moon on its right.

When the moth encounters a closer bright light, such as a lamp, its instincts tell it to do the same thing—that is, keep the lamp always on the right. Of course, the only way a moth can do this is to fly in a circle around the lamp.

—elephants are said to have good memories?

This reputation was earned both in India, where it was discovered that elephants could remember long lists of commands, and in Africa where elephants were known to be able to remember complicated routes to distant watering holes.

Experiments in the mid-1950s by B. Rensch, a German zoologist, confirmed that, although elephants are rather slow to learn, they do, in fact, have better-than-average memories.

Ever Wonder Why?

—hair growing in front of the ears is referred to as "sideburns"?

Sideburns got their name from General Ambrose Everett Burnside, Commander of the Union Army of the Potomac during the Civil War. General Burnside had long whiskers down the sides of his face in front of his ears. When others grew similar whiskers, they were said to be sporting "burnsides," a term that somehow got turned around and became "sideburns."

—cowboys sing?

Cowboys began singing to soothe their cattle. At night, when cattle have to remain stationary for long periods, they tend to get restless and want to mill around. Cowboys found that singing to the cattle calms them.

—public coaches in the early West were called "stagecoaches"?

Because journeys in these coaches were made in stages to allow tired horses to be replaced with fresh ones.

—saltine crackers have those 13 little holes in them?

The holes are put there by 13 docker pins used in the baking process, and the purpose of the holes is to allow all gases produced during baking to escape. If the holes were not there, the cracker would puff up into one big blister.

Ever Wonder Why?

—Tombstone, Arizona is named that?

During the 1800s, a gold prospector in Arizona named Ed Schieffelin stated his intention to begin prospecting in hostile Indian territory. "All you'll find is your own tombstone," he was told. But Ed persisted, and the territory he prospected came to be known as Ed Schieffelin's tombstone. Ed did not find gold, but he did find huge deposits of silver. Other prospectors rushed to the area, a new town was established and—since it had no other name—it was called "Tombstone," Arizona.

—getting a reprimand from the boss is referred to as "being called on the carpet"?

This expression originated in the days of the early railroad when executives had very plush offices and lower level workers had very little at all. When an employee was called to an executive office, he was said to be "called on the carpet"—the carpet being that covering the floor before the desk where the employee would stand. Later, the expression was applied almost exclusively to cases where an employee was receiving a reprimand.

—a bell, a book, and a candle are the symbols of excommunication?

The *bell* symbolizes the means of notifying the parishioners that the excommunication is about to take place; the *book* represents the book from which the sentence will be read; and the extinguished *candle* symbolizes the external darkness in which the excommunicated person must now dwell.

Ever Wonder Why?

—Mother's Day is on the second Sunday in May?
This day was chosen because it was on the second Sunday in May, 1908, that a special memorial service was held for Mrs. Anna Reeves Jarvis. Mrs. Jarvis was the mother of Anna M. Jarvis, the lady whose campaigning was primarily responsible for our national recognition of Mother's Day.

—the large, canvas-covered, curved wagons of the early West were called Conestoga wagons?
Because they were first built for use on farms in the Conestoga Valley of Pennsylvania. The wagons were curved to keep the cargo from sliding out when the wagon went uphill.

—eating ice cream too fast gives you a headache?
There is presently no certainty as to why this happens, but there are two theories:

1. The ice cream chills the soft palate on the roof of the mouth, causing a sudden flurry of nerve impulses to be sent to the brain stem located at the top of the spinal cord. The brain stem serves as a sort of headache center, and this sudden rush of impulses makes it think something is wrong in the head. In reaction to this, the brain stem sends out pain signals, producing the headache.

2. The cold ice cream causes blood vessels in the head to constrict, reducing the volume of blood flow, thereby causing the pain.

A more certain answer will have to await further research.

Ever Wonder Why?

—getting married is referred to as "tying the knot"?

There was a time when marriage ceremonies were not performed by the clergy, but by a member of the bride or groom's family—usually the male head of the family. The ceremonies were very brief and were concluded by tying together the sleeves of the marrying couple. This is the knot referred to in the expression "tying the knot."

—fooling someone is said to be "pulling the wool over his eyes"?

It was once customary for judges to wear wigs so large and cumbersome that they sometimes slipped down over the judge's eyes, making it difficult for him to see. These wigs were usually made of wool, and when a lawyer succeeded in tricking or deceiving a judge, it was said, jokingly, that he had "pulled the wool over the judge's eyes." Hence, the expression.

—bowling lanes are called "alleys"?

The term "alley" comes from the fact that the game was once played in the alleyways between houses or buildings.

Ever Wonder Why?

—the word "arms" is used so often in the names of hotels and apartment buildings?

During a time when many people were unable to read, inns and taverns had to be identified with signs containing pictures rather than words. This resulted in establishments with names like The Crown and Feather, the Golden Dove, and the Sword and Shield.

In many instances, when a famous person stayed at an inn, or perhaps lived near it, the proprietor of the inn named the inn after the person and used the person's coat of arms on its sign. This produced names like the Saxerby Arms, the King's Arms, and so forth.

These high-sounding names appealed to hotel and apartment owners in other parts of the world, and these owners soon began naming their own establishments in a similar manner.

—to "hightail it" means to depart quickly?

Trappers in the early West noticed that, when wild animals such as mustangs and rabbits are spooked, they raise their tails high in the air and speed away. This led to their describing any fast departure as "hightailing it."

—why it was once believed that garlic had the power to drive away vampires?

It has been suggested that the reason for this is *similia similibus curantur*—that is, similar things are cured by similar things, which is a long-winded way of saying fight fire with fire. Since vampires, being corpses, were presumed to smell bad, it was believed they would be repelled by something that smelled equally as bad. Hence the use of garlic.

Ever Wonder Why?

—trying to make a good impression is often described as "putting one's best foot forward"?

It would be putting it mildly to say that European noblemen of the past were preoccupied with their personal appearance. This is evidenced by their wigs, ruffled sleeves, fancy collars, tight breeches, shiny buttons, and colorful stockings. Of particular concern to this group was the shape of their legs, since the tight breeches and stockings tended to show them off. Since most men believed that one of their legs was formed a bit more perfectly than the other, when they stood in the presence of others, they tried to stand with "their best leg (or foot) forward."

—a dependable companion is called a "sidekick"?

The story behind this term is quite unusual and far from what one might guess.

The term "sidekick" comes from a pickpocket's jargon, and it means the front pocket in a pair of men's trousers. It is considered the hardest pocket to pick, since it is always in motion and because the man's hand is constantly swinging back and forth past it. It is, therefore, the safest and most dependable place for a man to carry his wallet. Somehow this idea of dependability came to be associated with a trusty companion, and the same term was used to describe him.

Ever Wonder Why?

—some say oysters should be eaten only in months with an "R" in their names?

The "R" months are September through April, which leaves only the hotter months May through August. Oysters are extra watery during hot weather, and this apparently led some to believe they weren't fit to eat during the hot months. This is not true, however, and oysters can be eaten at any time.

—a mischievous person is called a "Peck's bad boy"?

"Peck" was George Wilbur Peck, a Wisconsin newspaper editor, and his "bad boy" was Hennery, a fictional character Peck wrote about in a weekly newspaper column in the late 19th century. Hennery was a vicious prankster who played cruel tricks and practical jokes on his hapless father, which led to his being called "Peck's bad boy," a term that now applies to anyone of a similar nature.

—a place with as much snow as Greenland was named GREENland?

Eric the Red, who discovered the island, wanted other Norwegians to settle there, so he named the place Greenland to make it sound attractive. A clear case of false advertising!

Ever Wonder Why?

—on a hot day, you sometimes see what looks like a pool of water in the road ahead?

When a ray of light passes from a layer of cool air into a layer of warmer air, the ray is bent. This is called refraction. You can see the effects of refraction by observing what happens to the image of a pencil placed in a glass of clear water.

On a hot day, when the sun heats the surface of the road, the hot pavement heats the layer of air just above the road. When light from the sky enters this layer of hot air, the light is bent upward, as illustrated below:

A person in a position to see this bent light will see what is actually a reflection of the sky, but to him it will look like a bit of water in the road.

—Brooklyn's original baseball team was called the "Dodgers"?

In the days when trolly car lines crisscrossed most of Brooklyn, the residents of Brooklyn were nicknamed "trolly dodgers" or just "dodgers." So, when Brooklyn put together its baseball team, it was natural to call them the Brooklyn Dodgers.

Ever Wonder Why?

—Henry Ford's highly successful automobile was called the "Model T"?

When Ford began building automobiles in 1903, he decided to designate each different model—including the successes and the failures—using a letter of the alphabet. His big success was with his twentieth model, the one assigned the twentieth letter of the alphabet—"T." Hence the popular "Model T" Ford.

—The Italians named one of their traditional dances, the tarantella, after a spider?

Contrary to popular belief, the tarantella didn't get its name directly from the tarantula spider.

The tarantella, the tarantula, and a nervous disorder known as tarantism all take their name from the town of Taranto, Italy. At one time in that town, it was erroneously believed that tarantism was caused by the bite of the tarantula spider. It was further believed that a person suffering from tarantism could be cured only by dancing vigorously until all of the spider's venom had been sweated out. The fast whirling dance invented to effect this cure was given the name tarantella, after the name of the town, not the name of the spider.

Ever Wonder Why?

—so many taxicabs are yellow?

The largest taxi company in the world was started in 1907 by John D. Hertz, the same Hertz that founded Hertz Rent-A-Car. Because Hertz had read a University of Chicago study saying that yellow is the most visible of all colors, he decided that his cabs should be yellow. He eventually named his company the Yellow Cab Company, and yellow became the color most often chosen for taxis by other cab companies throughout the United States.

—a policeman is called a "cop"?

The word "cop" is not, as some believe, derived from the copper buttons once worn by English bobbies. The term "cop" predates the English bobby by 125 years. "Cop" comes from the Latin word *capere* meaning to seize or capture.

—churches have bells?

For a long time, it was widely believed that the sound of a bell could ward off evil, so bells were placed in churches to keep away bad spirits.

Ever Wonder Why?

—some men's dress shirts have those little loops near the center of the back?

These are called "locker loops," and they were put there so the shirt could be hung on the type of hook found in lockers. It is very difficult to otherwise hang a shirt with a stiff collar on such a hook.

—Mona Lisa has no eyebrows?

Because at the time da Vinci painted the picture, it was fashionable in Italy for women to pluck all of their eyebrows.

—we say "Hear! Hear!" when we approve of something someone is saying?

This expression originated in the British Parliament and was originally "Hear him! Hear him!" It meant, of course, "pay attention to what the speaker is saying." For brevity, it was shorted to just "Hear! Hear!"

—you often see bottles of colored water in the windows of pharmacies?

Originally, the bottles contained special preparations that required steeping, and they were set in the window so the sun's rays could accelerate the process. Later, when steeping was no longer done this way, pharmacists continued to put bottles of colored liquid in their windows to identify the pharmacy to the many people who, at that time, were unable to read.

Ever Wonder Why?

—MGM has a lion as its trademark?

The lion was the idea of Howard Dietz, the man in charge of advertising for Goldwyn Pictures. He got the idea from the picture of a lion on the cover of a campus publication of his alma mater, Columbia University. In 1924, when Goldwyn Pictures got together with Metro Studios and Louis B. Mayer to form MGM, they kept the lion as the new company's trademark.

—actors are wished good luck by telling them to "break a leg"?

At one time, it was believed that an evil presence watched over all events and took great delight in spoiling things most revered by man. At a horse race if a favorite horse was praised out loud, it was believed that the evil one might cause the horse to fall and break its leg. In an attempt to mislead the evil being, horse lovers began deliberately telling their horses to go ahead and "break a leg," while secretly wishing them good luck. It is this custom that accounts for the current usage in the theater. So as not to tempt evil fate, actors are now secretly wished good luck by telling them to "break a leg."

—the game Simon Says is called that?

The game was originally called "Do This, Do That," but when it became popular in New York's Catskill Mountains, it was renamed after a local social director who promoted it.

Ever Wonder Why?

—we say we wouldn't touch something with a 10-foot pole?

The 10-foot pole refers to the long pole once used by boatmen to push their boats along streams and rivers. The original idea was that there are some things a boatman might encounter (a large alligator, for instance) that would be too dangerous for him to touch even with his 10-foot pole.

—there is an eye in the top of a pyramid on a one-dollar bill?

The eye is supposed to symbolize an "all-seeing" deity, and the pyramid represents permanence and strength. The words *ANNUIT COEPTIS* above the pyramid mean "He (God) has favored us," and the words *NOVUS ORDO SECLORUM* below it mean "a new order of the ages." MDCCLXXVI written on the base of the pyramid is 1776 in Roman numerals.

—we say we slept "like a top"?

In the past, when a child's toy top was put away on a shelf or in a drawer for a while, it was said that the top was sleeping. This is where we get the expression "sleeping like a top."

Ever Wonder Why?

—you never see vitamin K in a multi-vitamin supplement?

One reason for this is that there is still some uncertainty about the daily requirement of vitamin K, since cases of vitamin K deficiency are extremely rare. A second reason is that vitamin K must be administered with great care, since too much can be toxic.

—when Yankee Doodle stuck a feather in his cap, he called it "macaroni"?

The macaroni in this song does not refer to pasta but to a social club popular in 18th century England called the Macaroni Club. The club's members were considered overdressed dandies, and Yankee Doodle was being described as one of these. The song was written by an Englishman to poke fun at the young, green American troops during the French and Indian War.

—very hot summer days are called "dog days"?

From July 3 to August 11, the Dog Star Sirius rises and sets with the sun. In early Rome, it was believed that the Dog Star was somehow responsible for the extremely hot weather during this period, and for this reason these very hot days were called *dies caniculares*, or days of the dog. This is why, today, we call hot summer days "dog days."

—June is such a popular month for weddings?

June was named after Juno, the wife of Jupiter and the goddess of marriage. At one time, it was believed that Juno gave her special blessings to women who married in the month named in her honor.

Ever Wonder Why?

—red and green are the traditional colors of Christmas?

We owe this tradition to the red berries and green leaves of the holly plant, which for centuries has been the most widely used Christmas decoration.

—a baby is sometimes smacked on the rump at birth?

When a baby is born, its oxygen supply is temporarily cut off and its respiratory tract is partially blocked by fluids. The smack on the rump makes the baby cry, thereby clearing the breathing passages and enabling the baby to take in the large quantities of air needed to get its lungs functioning.

—some Southerners are called "rednecks"?

In the beginning, the term was used to describe farm workers whose necks were usually red from working in the hot sun. Since then it has come to mean any working-class Southerner.

—in the lullaby "Rock-a-Bye Baby," the baby is in a treetop?

In colonial America, Indian mothers would sometimes hang their baby's birch bark cradle on the limb of a tree so the wind could gently rock it. It is said that a young man who came over on the Mayflower in 1620 observed this practice and was inspired to write the lullaby.

Ever Wonder Why?

—a raw steak is sometimes put on a black eye?
The discoloration of a black eye is due to blood from broken capillaries that has seeped into surrounding tissue. Since this blood is no longer supplied with the oxygen that gave it its red color, it turns blue, and when viewed through reddened skin, appears black.

Some of this discoloration can be prevented by placing something cold against the damaged area. The cold causes the blood vessels to constrict, thereby reducing the blood seepage.

At some point in the past, it was discovered that a raw steak right out of the refrigerator serves very well as the cold object. It is cold—but not too cold—and is flexible enough to fit snugly over the bruised eye.

—a collarless, pullover shirt is called a T-shirt?
It is so called because when it is laid flat, it is shaped like the letter "T."

—the Japanese remove their shoes before entering a dwelling?
At one time, the Japanese walked on, sat on, and slept on woven straw mats that covered the wooden floors in their homes. With age, these mats became brittle and could be damaged if walked on by someone wearing the wooden clogs popular at the time. To prevent such damage, the Japanese began removing their shoes before entering their homes.

Ever Wonder Why?

—an oboe is usually the first instrument you hear when an orchestra warms up?

Because the oboe is capable of emitting such a steady note and because the quality of the note is not very susceptible to variation due to temperature changes, other musicians use the oboe's "A" note to tune their own instruments. This is why you hear the oboe first.

—a promise of a reward in the remote future is called "pie in the sky"?

Joe Hill, an early twentieth century writer of songs about the working class, wrote a song in 1911 called "The Preacher and the Slave." In the song, Hill made fun of sermons that preach patience on the promise of rewards in the great hereafter.

This last line of the song is where we get the expression.

Ever Wonder Why?

—the sparks from a sparkler don't burn your hand?
While it is true that the sparks from a sparkler are, literally, as hot as fire, each spark is so tiny and exists for such a short time that the total amount of heat produced is not enough to cause a burn.

—we say "pleased as punch"?
The "punch" in the above saying refers to a puppet in the Punch and Judy puppet shows popular during the 17th and 18th centuries in Europe. Punch was an obnoxious and cruel character who badly mistreated his wife Judy and who was always portrayed as being exceptionally pleased with himself for doing so.

—agreeing to pay for something later is called buying "on the cuff"?
This saying originated in the taverns of the past where it was often customary for a bartender to write his customer's bar tabs on the large white cuffs of his shirt.

Ever Wonder Why?

—filmmakers always snap the top of that black and white board when a scene begins?

Filmmakers usually find it necessary to adjust the picture and sound portions of their films to make sure they are exactly matched, or synchronized. They do this so that when an actor's lips move or when a gun is fired, the sound is there at the right time. The black and white board, called a clapperboard, is used for this purpose. The top of the board is snapped shut as soon as the camera starts to roll, thus giving the filmmaker a frame at the very beginning of the film that can be used to syncronize the sound. He will adjust the film's sound track until the crisp snap of the clapperboard coincides exactly with the picture of the board being snapped shut.

The clapperboard also serves other purposes such as identifying the scene and the number of takes.

Ever Wonder Why?

—salt is put on icy roads?

The freezing point of water is the temperature at which the water will turn to ice. Above the freezing point, the water is a liquid; below the freezing point, it is ice. It follows then that if you could somehow lower the freezing point of water, you could make it remain a liquid at lower temperatures.

Now it is a fact of nature that when a substance is dissolved in water, it automatically lowers the freezing point of the water. And, this is true when salt is dissolved in water.

On an icy road, the surface of the ice is not always frozen, but is, in fact, continually melting and refreezing. When salt is put on the ice, it dissolves in the melted ice and lowers its freezing point. This means that the water will now remain a liquid at a lower temperature and not refreeze again. As more ice melts, more salt dissolves in the water, and more water is prevented from refreezing. Eventually, all of the ice is gone—replaced by water—and the road is safer to travel. This is why salt is put on an icy road.

As a final note, salt will work this way only when the temperature is just a few degrees below the normal freezing point of water (32°F or 0°C). At very low temperatures, the salt will not have this effect.

Ever Wonder Why?

—deception or trickery is often called "hocus pocus"?

During Catholic communion services, the priest holds up bread and says, "This is the body of the Lord." The Catholics believe that, at that moment, the bread is actually transformed into the body of Christ. This is known as the doctrine of transubstantiation.

In other religions, however, the bread is viewed only as a symbolic representation of the body of Christ and not as the actual body itself. People of these other religions have been known to ridicule the Catholics for their more extreme view.

When the priest says, "This is the body of the Lord" in Latin, it becomes "Hoc est corpus domini." People who don't hold to the doctrine of transubstantiation began referring to the Catholic doctrine as just a lot of "hoc est corpus." Over time, this was distorted to "hocus corpus" and finally to "hocus pocus." Since then the term has come to mean any kind of deliberate deception or trickery.

—a jackass is the symbol of the Democratic party and an elephant the symbol of the Republican party?

The jackass was the idea of Andrew Jackson, who chose it because his opponents had referred to him as a jackass during his 1828 presidential campaign. The elephant was the invention of cartoonist Thomas Nast, and he meant for the elephant to symbolize the Republican party's strength.

54

Ever Wonder Why?

—diamonds are used for engagement rings?

Maximilian I, Emperor of the Holy Roman Empire from 1493 to 1519, started this custom when he gave a diamond to his future wife, Mary of Burgundy, in 1477.

—we say "Eureka!" when we make a surprising discovery?

"Eureka" means "I have found it" in the language of ancient Greece. It became a popular expression because it was reportedly uttered by the Greek scientist Archimedes when he discovered the principle behind why things float. According to most accounts, Archimedes was taking a bath when he made the discovery and was so thrilled by it that he ran down the streets of Syracuse clad only in a towel shouting, "Eureka! Eureka!"

—people used to put *blue*ing into the wash to make their clothes *white*r?

For every primary color in the visible spectrum, there is another color known as its complement, and when light of one color is mixed with light of its complementary color, the result is white light.

When clothes—especially cotton clothes—become old, they often take on a yellowish hue. The color complement of yellow is blue. Therefore, when a blueing agent is added to the wash, it counteracts the yellow, producing whiter-looking clothes.

Blueing is no longer used, because although it did make clothes appear less yellow, it also produced a poor-quality white, one appearing almost gray. Today, flourescent whiteners are used instead.

Ever Wonder Why?

—a game of pocket billiards is called "pool"?

"Pool," in this case, refers to the pool of bets on the game. Players and onlookers in billiard parlors and other gambling houses used to place their wagers in a common pool when betting on a game. In fact, "poolroom" originally meant any gambling parlor, including the ones in which billiards were played. Seeing the game of billiards being played in places called poolrooms led some to mistakenly refer to the game itself as pool.

—carrots are rumored to be good for the eyes?

Carrots are a rich source of carotene, a substance that turns to vitamin A in the body. Since vitamin A is known to be essential for good night vision, this led to the conclusion that carrots must be good for the eyes.

—a depressed and irritable person is said to be in a "black" mood?

According to Greek thought around the 6th century B.C., a person's mood was determined by four bodily substances called humors. They were blood, phlegm, yellow bile, and black bile.

A person with more blood than anything else was thought to be sturdy, robust, and cheerful, or what we would now call sanguine. A person with an excess of phlegm was believed to be slow, dull, and unemotional. We would now call such a person phlegmatic. Someone with too much yellow bile was hot-tempered and violent—or choleric. And a person with too much black bile was presumed to be sad, depressed, and irritable. His personality would now be described as melancholic, and his mood described as black.

Ever Wonder Why?

—pigs wallow in mud?

Pigs do this to keep cool. Since they have no functional sweat glands and are, therefore, unable to sweat, pigs have had to find other means of lowering their body temperature. Wallowing in mud turns out to be an excellent way to do this. Mud cools both by evaporation and by conduction of heat into the cool ground, making it a more effective coolant than water.

—mesas are flat on top?

Mesas are the remains of larger plateaus that have partially worn away over time. The parts of the original plateau that have now vanished were made of substances such as shale and silt stone, substances unable to withstand the forces of erosion. The parts still standing are those made of substances such as lava and sandstone that are better able to resist erosion.

—small pocketknives are called penknives?

At one time, writing pens were made mostly of quills or reeds and had to be sharpened frequently. For this reason, people usually carried in their pockets small knives which they called their "penknives."

Ever Wonder Why?

—ice cream is served in cones?

The ice cream cone was a spur-of-the-moment idea. It was invented, quite by chance, at the 1904 World's Fair in St. Louis when an ice cream vendor named Fornachou ran out of paper plates. In the booth next to Fornachou, a Syrian baker named Hamwi was selling waffles. When Hamwi learned of Fornachou's problem, he suggested serving the ice cream on waffles! Fornachou liked the idea, but realized he couldn't serve ice cream on a flat waffle. The solution, of course, was to roll the waffle into a cone. They did this, and the ice cream cone was born.

—pretending to be sick or dead is referred to as "playing possum"?

When an opossum finds that it cannot fight or bluff its way out of a threatening situation, it will, upon occasion, fall into a coma and appear, from all outward signs, to be dead. Its body will become rigid, its respiration will slow almost to a stop, and its pulse will become imperceptible. This may, indeed, cause the aggressor to lose interest by convincing it that the opossum has just died, but scientists are not at all certain that the opossum does this deliberately. In any case, it is because of this reaction that we refer to various kinds of human pretending as "playing possum."

Ever Wonder Why?

—a bottle of champagne is broken on the prow of a ship at its launching?

In pagan times, a human life was often sacrificed at the launching of a new ship to ensure the ship's good fortune. When times became more civilized, the launching ceremony was changed to one involving the pouring of wine instead of blood on the vessel. Today, all that is left of this custom is the breaking of the bottle of champagne on the ship's prow.

—@ means "at"?

It is likely that @ is a graphic distortion of the Latin word ad, meaning "at." The distortion over time could have occurred as follows: ad @ @

—the twenty-third Psalm says "He leadeth me beside the STILL waters"?

In this Psalm, a comparison is being made to a shepherd leading his flock of sheep to a watering place. The Psalm says STILL waters, because sheep will not drink from moving water.

—you can't let go of an electric wire?

It is not because your hand sticks to the wire, but because the alternating electric current passing through your hand causes the muscles in the hand and arm to contract, forcing your fingers to close tightly around the wire.

Ever Wonder Why?

—marriage is called "wedlock"?

This word comes from two Anglo-Saxon words, "wed" meaning pledge and "lac" meaning gift. Originally, "wedlack" referred to gifts given by the bride's father to the groom in return for the groom's pledge to marry his daughter. Since that time, the word has become "wedlock" and has come to mean the marriage itself.

—"getting the sack" means getting fired?

There was a time when mechanics and other workmen used to bring their own sack of tools to the job. The tools were normally placed on the workman's bench and the sack left with their employer for safekeeping. When a workman was let go, he was given his final paycheck—and his sack. Thus, if someone "got the sack," it meant he had been fired.

—the Apostle's creed as spoken in *Protestant* ceremonies contains the statement, "I believe in the holy *catholic* church"?

The word "catholic" in this case means "universal." It does not refer to the Roman Catholic Church.

Ever Wonder Why?

—we write from left to right?

In ancient times, writing was done by inscribing pictures on small, clay tablets with a pointed instrument. The first of these tablets were small enough to be held in the palm of the hand, and in this position, it was natural for the writer to make the pictures one under the other, from top to bottom.

Eventually, however, the tablets grew in length until they could no longer be held in the hand, but had to be laid along the forearm. In this position, the pictures that had previously been written from top to bottom were now most conveniently written from left to right.

By the time the pictures evolved into letters, the habit of left-to-right writing had become firmly established.

Ever Wonder Why?

—when dice are rolled, seven comes up more than any other number?

When you roll a pair of dice, there are six ways the number seven can come up:

1st Die		2nd Die		
1	+	6	=	7
2	+	5	=	7
3	+	4	=	7
4	+	3	=	7
5	+	2	=	7
6	+	1	=	7

Since no other number has this many ways of being rolled, the number 7 always has a better chance of coming up than any other number.

—extra long writing paper is sometimes called "foolscap"?

The name comes from a watermark that used to appear on such paper. The watermark consisted of the cap and bells of an ancient jester, and it was originally placed on the long paper used for parliamentary journals in England. This was done by the British parliament under Cromwell as a way of protesting the fact that Charles I had given unfair monopoly privileges to certain paper manufacturers he favored. Charles eventually had the watermark removed but not before this size paper had gained the nickname "foolscap."

Ever Wonder Why?

—Michelangelo's statue of Moses has horns?

The horns are the result of a Biblical misinterpretation. In Hebrew, the same word means both a "radiated" head and a "horned" head, and while the original writer was trying to describe Moses as having rays of light coming from his head, a Bible translator mistook the words to mean that Moses had horns. Guided by this translation, Michelangelo gave Moses horns.

—"moxie" means nerve or courage?

"Moxie" was the name of a soft drink popular around 1876. Its distributors advertised it as a tonic that would build up one's nerve, and because of this image, a courageous person was soon described as one "having a lot of moxie."

Ever Wonder Why?

—extreme cold causes lips to turn blue?

Lips are normally red because they contain a large number of capillaries. Under conditions of extreme cold, blood vessels in the body constrict, reducing the flow of blood, and hence the amount of oxygen, that reaches the capillaries in the lips. When blood is thus deprived of oxygen, it turns a deeper color which appears blue under the skin, and this is what gives the lips their bluish color.

—babies are given rattles as toys?

The earliest rattles—which go back to 2500 B.C.— were given to babies not to amuse them but to ward off evil spirits. It was believed that the loud noise the rattles made would protect the baby by scaring away demons.

—some types of attempted deception are referred to as "mumbo jumbo"?

Mumbo Jumbo, originally pronounced "ma-ma-dy-umbo," was the name of a West African tribal priest who, according to legend, could perform great magic. It is reported that tribesmen who were having trouble with their wives would sometimes hire a friend to dress up and act like Mumbo Jumbo in an attempt to frighten their wives into obedience. This type of deception soon came to be called "mumbo jumbo," and later, the term was generalized to include other types of trickery.

Ever Wonder Why?

**—the moon often looks orange or red when it is low
on the horizon?**

White light, such as that coming from the moon, is
composed of all the colors of the spectrum from the
short wavelength colors on the blue-green end to the
long wavelength colors on the red-orange end.

When the moon is low on the horizon, its light has to
pass through more of the earth's atmosphere to reach
the viewer's eye, meaning that it will encounter more of
those things in the atmosphere that tend to scatter the
shorter wavelength colors such as blue and green.
Therefore, by the time the light reaches the viewer's
eye, the blue and green colors have been scattered out,
leaving only the long wavelength colors, such as red
and orange. This is what gives the moon its orange
color.

—Christmas is celebrated on December 25?

Of course, no one knows exactly when Christ was
born. The date December 25 was chosen because, oddly
enough, that day had been a pagan holiday.

December 25 was once called the Day of the Invinci-
ble Sun, and it was a day dedicated to the pagan god
Mithras. When the Emperor Constantine ordered that
Christianity replace paganism in the 4th century A.D.,
the Christians elected to celebrate Christ's birthday on
that same day as a way of showing that Christ had replaced Mithras.

Ever Wonder Why?

—the caduceus is the symbol of the medical profession?

Hermes, messenger of the gods, carried a caduceus and, with it, was supposed to have been able to bring people back to earth from hell. The caduceus was also carried by messengers in ancient Greece as a symbol that the messenger was on a peaceful mission. It is speculated that because of these two roles of the caduceus, the medical profession chose to adopt it as its symbol.

—the moon looks larger when it is near the horizon?
This effect is actually an optical illusion. The visual image of the moon is exactly the same size on the horizon as it is any other place in the sky. It looks larger on the horizon because it appears nearer to things of known size—such as buildings and trees—to which it can be compared.

Ever Wonder Why?

—you see stars when you are hit on the head?

The back of the eye contains millions of special nerve cells that detect light and send signals to the brain telling it of the presence of the light. When the head is struck, these nerve cells are jolted, causing them to send erroneous signals. When the signals are received by the brain, they are interpreted as tiny points of light, causing the person struck to think he is seeing stars.

—on a very hot day, the surface of the road ahead seems to be shimmering?

When the sun heats the road's pavement, the pavement heats the layer of air just above it. This causes the air just above the road to rise, and as this hot air rises, cooler air moves in to take its place. The hot pavement then heats this air, causing it to rise, and the process repeats itself. As a result of all of this, the layer of air just above the surface of a hot road is in constant motion. When light passes through this mixture of hot and cool moving air, the light's rays are bent in constantly changing directions. When you look up ahead and view the surface of the road through this layer of moving air, the changing light makes the road appear to shimmer.

Ever Wonder Why?

—some children's stories are called Mother Goose stories?

Queen Bertha, wife of Pepin the Short and mother of Charlemagne, was rumored to have had webbed feet, and for this reason was called Queen Goosefoot.

In pictures of Bertha, she is often shown sitting at her spinning wheel telling stories to children seated around her. It has been suggested that this portrayal of Queen Goosefoot led some to refer to her as Mother Goose and to her tales as Mother Goose stories.

With the passage of time, many types of children's stories were called Mother Goose stories, and it was upon hearing one of these that French author Charles Perrault decided to write a collection of stories and call them *Tales of Mother Goose*. It was Perrault's book, published in 1697, that popularized the term "Mother Goose." On the book's front piece was the picture of an old woman, very reminiscent of Queen Bertha, seated at a spinning wheel.

—there is always a wad of cotton in new bottles of pills?

The cotton is to keep the pills from bouncing around and getting chipped during shipment.

Ever Wonder Why?

—it was once believed that holding one's breath could keep one from being stung by a bee?

People who believed this knew that a bee stings by sticking its stinger into a pore. They believed that holding one's breath would cause the pores to shut tight, making it impossible for the bee to insert its stinger. This, of course, is not true.

—John Hancock signed his name so large on the Declaration of Independence?

He wanted to make certain that the nearsighted King George III could read the signature without his glasses.

—when a person who had given up alcohol starts to drink again, we say that he has "fallen off the wagon"?

In the late 1800s, a time when water was hauled around in horse-drawn wagons, a man who had decided to refrain from strong drink was said to have climbed aboard the water wagon. Later, if the man returned to drinking, he was said to have "fallen off the wagon."

—you can hear the sound of the surf in a seashell?

The roaring sound is a mixture of the various sounds around the shell, including the sound of blood pulsing in the listener's ear. The smooth, curved walls of the shell's interior caused the sound waves to be bounced around, blended, and magnified in such a way that, when they emerge from the shell, they sound like the surf.

Ever Wonder Why?

—Chinese men used to wear long pigtails?

When the Mongolian people of Manchuria conquered China in 1644, the Chinese men were made to shave their heads in an act of submission. The men were allowed, however, to keep hair on the backs of their heads but were required to keep it braided in a pigtail. By the time the Chinese took back their country in 1912, the pigtails had become so popular that the men chose to keep them.

—a chess player says "checkmate" when he captures his opponent's king?

Chess originated in India in the 7th century A.D., and its popularity quickly spread to Persia. The Persian word for "king" is "shah," and the phrase "shah mat" means, "the king is dead." This—with some distortion in pronunciation—is where we get the term "checkmate."

—rough comedy is called "slapstick"?

A "slapstick" was, in fact, a stick. It was made of two flat pieces of wood that slapped together loudly when it was struck against something. In early comedy theater, the slapstick was used by stage comedians to strike their hapless victims in rough comedy skits. Eventually, this type of skit was called slapstick comedy.

Ever Wonder Why?

—people sometimes extend their little finger when they eat or drink?

Around the 13th century A.D. it was common practice for diners to eat meat with their fingers. In order to keep a couple of fingers grease-free for handling bread and other dishes, the diners held the fingers in an extended position. It is believed that this may account for the current practice of extending the pinkie.

—a loan shark is called a "shylock"?

"Shylock" is the name of a cruel money lender in Shakespeare's *Merchant of Venice*, who lent money to the merchant Antonio and demanded a pound of his flesh in return.

—turkeys have the reputation of being stupid?

Farmers formed this opinion of turkeys after observing that very young domestic turkeys apparently "don't know enough to come in out of the rain."

For the first few weeks of their lives, baby turkeys have to be herded to shelter by their mothers when it rains. If the mother turkeys fail to do this—as sometimes happens with domestic turkeys—the baby turkeys might remain outside in a downpour and drown.

Ever Wonder Why?

—singer Ernest Evans calls himself Chubby Checker?

He patterned his name after another singer he greatly admired, Fats Domino. Chubby (Fats) Checker (Domino).

—the place to which the tornado carried Dorothy was named "Oz"?

According to Lyman Baum, author of *The Wizard of Oz*, he got the idea for the name from an office file drawer labeled "O-Z."

—hailstones get so large?

During a hailstorm, droplets of water turn to ice at high altitudes where the temperature of the air is below the freezing point of water. As these frozen droplets start to fall toward earth, they pass through warmer altitudes and collect layers of water on their surfaces. Some of the droplets are then caught in strong updrafts and carried back up to the colder altitudes, where the new layers of water freeze, making the balls of ice a little larger. These refrozen balls then start to fall again, gain another layer of water, and are carried, once again, back up to the colder regions to be refrozen. This process continues until the ball of ice is too heavy to be lifted by the updraft, and at this point, the ball falls to earth as a hailstone. The size of the hailstone, therefore, is determined by how many trips it makes back up into the colder region.

Ever Wonder Why?

—mercury is used in thermometers?

After trying other liquids, such as water and alcohol, mercury was chosen as the best liquid to use in thermometers for the following reasons: (1) it will not freeze at temperatures above -38°F, (2) it does not wet—and, therefore, stick to—the inner walls of the thermometer, and (3) its great surface tension prevents it from sliding back down the tube after the temperature has been measured. This latter property, incidentally, is why you have to "shake down" a thermometer before using it.

—an offspring is sometimes called the "spitting image" of a parent?

This is, most probably, a southern contraction of the phrase "spirit and image," as in "the son is the very spirit and image of his father."

—salty foods make you thirsty?

The human body will tolerate only a fixed ratio of salt to water in its bodily fluids. When you eat salty foods, you increase this ratio beyond what the body will allow. To return the ratio to the correct level, the body demands more water, and this is what makes you thirsty.

—the number 13 is considered unlucky?

The most frequently encountered explanation of this superstition attributes it to the fact that there were 13 people—Christ and his 12 apostles—at the Last Supper.

Ever Wonder Why?

—that famous movie vampire was named "Dracula"?

Movies about Dracula are based on a book written by Bram Stoker in 1897. Stoker named the evil vampire in his book Dracula after a real person who lived in the mid-15th century.

Vlad Tepes, also known as Vlad the Impaler, was governor of Wallachia in Transylvania around 1456. Vlad was not a vampire, but a cruel, sadistic ruler who brutally tortured and killed his enemies by impaling them on sharp, wooden spikes. Monks, who wrote about Vlad, called him "Dracula," which means "devil" in Romanian. It was these accounts of the real Dracula that led to Bram Stoker's book and the name he gave to his vampire.

—an actor who overacts is called a "ham"?

Actors used to put ham fat under their makeup to make it easier to remove. This led to actors being called, first, "hamfatters" and then "hams." At some point, the term "ham" came to describe one who over-acts.

Ever Wonder Why?

—the trousers of the army's dress blue uniform are several shades lighter than the jacket?

It is commonly told that the two shades of blue came about during the hot days of the Indian campaigns when soldiers on horseback often removed their jackets and tucked them into their saddlebags when they were out of sight of the fort. This caused the trousers to be bleached by the sun at a faster rate than the jackets, making them a lighter blue. This gave formations a mottled look, and to correct the problem, the army decided to make all trousers a lighter shade of blue. So goes the popular explanation. In truth, however, the color difference is due to the fact that different kinds of fabrics were used to make the trousers and jackets of the early uniforms, and different dyes were found to be most suitable for the two types of fabric. Of course, once the two-toned pattern had been established, it became the standard.

—actors consider it bad luck to wear anything green onstage?

In the earlier days of the theater, green lights, called limelights, were used to spotlight important happenings onstage. In this light, an actor's green clothes had a tendency to "wash out," making the actor less noticeable. Being less noticeable was considered very unlucky for an actor, and hence the taboo against green costumes.

Ever Wonder Why?

—sweet talk and flattery are called "blarney"?

It is told that in the year 1602 in the town of Blarney in County Cork, an Irish nobleman named Cormack McCarthy found his castle surrounded by British troops poised for attack. The attack never took place, however, because McCarthy was able to sweet-talk the British commander into postponing the siege indefinitely. Since this took place in Blarney, smooth talk was henceforth described by that name.

—we speak of "knocking the tar" out of someone?

At one time, when sheep were accidentally cut during shearing, tar was put on the wound to prevent infection. This tar then clung to the wool and had to be removed before the wool could be sold. The removal process usually consisted of "beating the tar" out of the wool. Hence, the expression.

—that famous sportswear company is named ADIDAS?

Contrary to what you may have heard, the letters do not stand for All Day I Dream About Shoes! The company was started in 1920 by a German entrepreneur named Adolph Dassler, whose nickname was Adi. When it came time to select a name for his company, he used his nickname plus the first three letters of his last name.

Ever Wonder Why?

—certain newspaper reporters are called "stringers"?

In the early days of the newspaper business, freelance reporters were often paid according to the number of inches of type their stories contained. To determine how much they were owed, the reporters used to cut out each line of their story and paste them all together in a long string so the total length could be measured. Reporters who did this were referred to as "stringers."

—the Shell Oil Company chose a seashell as its trademark?

The big oil company began as a small shop in London that sold seashells. In 1897, the small company, called "The Shell Shop," began selling barreled kerosene as a side line. This part of the business turned out to be a tremendous success, and the company changed its name to the Shell Transport and Trading Company. As the petroleum business continued to grow, the company retained the name Shell and eventually became the Shell Oil Company. In 1904, the company made a scallop shell its trademark.

—mosquitoes hum?

The humming sound is caused by the high-speed flutter of the mosquito's wings. The pitch of the male's hum is slightly different from that of the female's. This enables the males and females to locate each other during the mating season.

Ever Wonder Why?

—a bell is often hung on a cat's collar?
The bell is to prevent the cat from sneaking up on an unsuspecting bird.

—dock workers are called "longshoremen"?
Because they work *along*-the-*shore*. In fact, they were originally called "along shore" men.

—laundry detergent brighteners make clothes look brighter?
Laundry brighteners are fluorescent substances that reflect some of the sun's invisible ultraviolet radiation as a pale blue light. When clothes are washed with a detergent containing a brightener, some of the fluourescent substance sticks to the fabric causing it to, literally, glow in the sun's light.

—the pupils of a cat's eyes become vertical slits in bright light?
A cat's eyes are structured to enable the cat to see in almost total darkness. Eyes that can do this are, understandably, extremely sensitive to light and must be protected against too much light. The slit pupils enable the cat to better restrict the amount of light that enters the eye. The fact that the slits are vertical allow the light to be reduced even further when the cat partially closes its eyelids.

Ever Wonder Why?

—clear adhesive tape is called "Scotch" tape?

In this case, the word "Scotch" means tight-fisted and stingy.

When this type of tape was first manufactured, it had adhesive only along the edges. It was assumed that this was done to save money, so the tape was nicknamed "Scotch" tape. Apparently, the manufacturer didn't object to the image this portrayed, because it decided to market the tape under that name.

—salt is put on the ice in an ice cream freezer?

When ice melts, it absorbs heat from the things around it, making them cold. When salt is put on the ice in an ice cream freezer, it causes the ice to melt, thereby absorbing heat from the ice cream, making it cold enough to freeze.

Ever Wonder Why?

—a man's tailless jacket for evening wear is called a "tuxedo"?

The tuxedo gets its name from the Tuxedo Park Country Club near Tuxedo Lake, New York where, in 1886, a club member named Griswold Lorillard attended a white-tie-and-tail affair wearing a black, tailless coat with satin lapels. He explained his attire by saying that it was a formal smoking jacket fashionable in Great Britain at that time. The new style jacket became popular and was given the name of the club where it was first introduced.

—a gentleman walks on the street-side of a lady?

This was done to prevent the lady from being splattered by horses, wagons, or other vehicles passing along the street.

—Ivory soap floats?

It floats because it is full of air. During the manufacturing process, tiny air bubbles are released into the soap mixture.

The first time this happened, it was purely by accident. A negligent employee allowed the soap to remain in the stirring stage too long, and this introduced air bubbles into the soap mixture. Top management wasn't told about this, and the soap was shipped to customers, who immediately wrote back saying how much they liked the new floating soap.

Ever Wonder Why?

—"lock, stock, and barrel" means completely?
In the days of the musket, a rifle consisted of a lock (the firing mechanism), a stock (the body of the rifle), and a barrel. Thus, "lock, stock, and barrel" meant a complete rifle, and with time, it came to mean a complete anything.

—we wink?
According to theory, when the eye closes in a wink, it represents something hidden, some sort of secret that can't be seen by most. Therefore, when you wink at someone, you are indicating that there exists an unspoken secret between you. When the wink is at someone of the opposite sex, the secret is implied to be of a sexual nature.

—the Bronx is called that?
The region now called the Bronx was once a farm owned by a man named Jonas Bronck. People going to the farm for a visit said they were going to the Bronck's, just as they would have said to the Smith's or to the Brown's. After the property was no longer a farm and no longer belonged to Jonas Bronck, people still referred to it as the Broncks. Eventually the spelling was distorted to Bronx.

Ever Wonder Why?

—your ears pop when you go up in an airplane?
Normally, the air pressure on either side of the eardrum is the same, but when you fly, the air pressure in the cabin drops, causing the pressure on the outside of the ear to be lower than that on the inside. This difference in pressure causes the eardrum to bulge outward, producing the tightness you feel just before your ears pop. When you swallow, your eustachian tube widens slightly, and this lowers the pressure on the inside, making it the same as that on the outside. When this happens, it causes the eardrum to "pop" back into place.

—the international society for the relief of suffering chose a Red Cross as its symbol?
The Red Cross organization was founded in Geneva, Switzerland in 1864 by Jean Dunant. It was decided to use a red cross on a white background as the organization's emblem in honor of the country in which it was founded. Switzerland's flag is a white cross on a red background.

—the Baby Ruth candy bar was given that name?
The candy bar was not named after Babe Ruth but after Baby Ruth Cleveland, daughter of Grover Cleveland.

Ever Wonder Why?

—you can get the German measles only once?

When a threatening virus attacks your body, the body responds by producing millions of antibodies specifically designed to destroy the virus and remove it from your system. When the virus is gone, many of the antibodies stay behind and prevent the same virus from growing in your body again. This is why you don't have to worry about getting some diseases like the German measles more than once.

—very small towns are called "jerkwater" towns?

In the days of the steam locomotive, trains often stopped at very small towns for no other reason than to take on water. When the train had positioned itself next to the water tower in one of these towns, a crewman would "jerk" a chain that lowered a long water spigot down into the train's tender. Hence the term, "jerkwater" town.

—the color green is sometimes considered unlucky?

In ancient times, many of our ancestors believed that green spirits lived underground and were responsible for making plants grow and for making them green. It was also believed that these spirits didn't take kindly to anyone besides themselves making things green. So, not wishing to anger these spirits, our ancestors avoided the color green, and this is what led to the superstition.

Ever Wonder Why?

—a gorilla beats his chest?

It was once believed that, when a gorilla stands up and beats his chest, it is because he is angry and about to attack. Today, scientists no longer believe this. In fact, chest-beating is now viewed as a way of avoiding hostilities.

When a male gorilla puffs out his chest and pounds it loudly with his cupped hands, he is announcing his location and identifying his domain. And while the gorilla is not threatening an immediate attack, he is warning animals in the area not to trespass. If the other animals take heed of the warning, then the chest-beating will have prevented a physical confrontation and preserved the peace.

—making a blunder means you might have to "eat crow"?

One explanation of this expression goes back to the War of 1812 when an American soldier, out to do some hunting, was said to have blundered into British territory during a temporary truce. The soldier didn't have a good day, though, and was able to bag only a crow. He was also unlucky in another way. His shot was heard by a British soldier who caught him and made him eat part of the crow. Word of the incident got around and, before long, it became commonplace to tell anyone caught in a blunder that he or she must now "eat crow."

Ever Wonder Why?

—golf balls have dimples?

Golf balls were originally made with smooth surfaces, but it was soon noticed that balls tended to travel further when their surfaces became scarred. The reason for this is as follows:

When a smooth ball travels through the air, the layer of air next to the ball flows around it, forming swirls or vortices, but does not flow into the area directly behind the ball. This creates a low-pressure area behind the ball which tends to pull the ball backward.

With a scarred ball, the rough surface tends to disturb the layer of air flowing around the ball causing more air to flow directly behind it. This causes less of a low-pressure area in the rear, meaning that the rough-surface ball is not pulled back as much as the smooth ball. This is what allows the rough-surface ball to travel farther, and this is why dimples were put on the surfaces of golf balls.

—flowers are sent to funerals?

This custom comes from a time when it was believed that a deceased person could get into Heaven only if that person had been highly regarded on earth. Displaying flowers at a funeral was one way to show that the dearly departed was, in fact, well-respected.

—the Confederate flag has 13 stars when only 11 states seceded from the Union?

The two extra stars represent Kentucky and Missouri, who hadn't seceded but who were counted because they were represented in the Confederate Congress.

Ever Wonder Why?

—Cinderella's slippers were made of glass?

The familiar story of Cinderella was written by the French author Charles Perrault in 1729 and published in his book, *Tales of Mother Goose*. This was not, however, the first time this story had been told. There are, in fact, over five hundred versions of the story going back to the 9th century A.D., and in the earlier versions, the slippers are not made of glass. Also, in these earlier versions, the prince is often tricked by the wicked stepmother into marrying one of the ugly daughters first. To deceive the prince, the wicked stepmother cut off the toes of one of her ugly daughters to make the daughter's foot fit into the slippers. The prince was fooled and married the daughter. Later, when he discovered the deception, he returned the ugly daughter and married his true love.

Perrault apparently considered this a needless complication and decided to make it impossible for the prince to be fooled in this way. So he made the slippers glass so the prince could see right through them.

—Coca Cola is named that?

The name comes from two of the beverage's principal ingredients: extract of coca leaves and extract of cola nuts.

—sailors began wearing tattoos?

Sailors began wearing tattoos so their bodies could be identified should they be killed in a shipwreck. Catholic sailors often wore the tattoo of a crucifix to ensure that they would receive proper burial rites.

Ever Wonder Why?

—an acceleration race between cars is called a "drag" race?

"Drag" is another name for street, as in the expression "main drag." Since the first acceleration races were run on drags, they were called "drag races."

Streets may be called "drags" because in the days of dirt streets, the streets were leveled by "dragging," that is, by pulling a heavy wooden frame (called a drag) up and down the street.

—you see blue sparks when you chew a wintergreen mint in a dark room?

All matter, including candy mints, is electrical in nature, and in the case of wintergreen mints, this electrical nature produces an unusual effect.

When you bite into a wintergreen mint and crack the mint crystals, opposite electrical charges are formed on either side of the crack line. This causes an electrical charge to jump from one side of the crack to the other, producing the bluish spark you see. This phenomenon is known as triboluminescence, and its effect can also be seen by rapidly unrolling certain types of adhesive tape in total darkness.

—we say "still waters run deep"?

The expression means, of course, that a quiet person often has strong feelings deep inside. The analogy is to a stream of water. A stream that is very deep flows by with relative quiet, or stillness, while a shallow stream, bubbling over rocks, makes a great deal of noise.

87

Ever Wonder Why?

—high quality writing or typing paper often has a watermark?

Paper manufacturers began using watermarks in the 13th century to display their trademarks and to serve as a guarantee of quality.

—an actor's backstage waiting room is called a "green room"?

When actors are onstage, the glare of the artificial lighting puts a strain on their eyes. To help relieve some of the strain, it became customary to paint the walls of the actor's waiting room green, green being a very restful color to the eyes. For this reason, such waiting rooms became known as "green rooms."

—the Irish wear a shamrock on St. Patrick's Day?

Saint Patrick was a missionary who, in the 5th century A.D., converted the Irish to Christianity. It is said that he illustrated the Holy Trinity—the father, the son, and the holy ghost—with a 3-leaf clover, or shamrock. For this reason, shamrocks have become part of St. Patrick's Day celebrations.

—croissants are crescent-shaped?

In 1863, the Ottoman Turks attempted to occupy the city of Vienna, Austria but were repelled by the brave Viennese people. To commemorate the victory, a baker in Vienna created a new pastry—the croissant—and shaped it like the crescent on the Turkish flag. Eating the pastry, he thought, would remind the Viennese of the "bite they had taken out of the Turkish army."

Ever Wonder Why?

—it was once advised that credit cards should never be carried in eelskin wallets?

Most credit cards have a magnetic strip on the back that carries certain information about the cardholder. It is known that exposing this strip to an electric field could destroy the information. Since some eels are capable of producing an electric current, it was believed that the eelskin in a wallet might still contain enough of the eel's electrical property to ruin the information on the magnetic strip. This is why it was once said that credit cards should not be carried in wallets made of eelskin.

This is not a real concern, however, since the types of eel used in making eelskin wallets are not the type that generate electric currents. And even if electric eels were used to make the wallets, there would still be no danger, since any remnants of the eel's electrical properties would be completely neutralized during the manufacturing process.

—"23 skiddoo" means "beat it"?

"Skiddoo" probably comes from an older word "skiddle," meaning to "move away quickly," and the "23" may refer to the 23rd Avenue in New York City.

In the early 1900s, it is said that young men used to gather in front of the Flatiron Building at Broadway and 23rd Avenue on windy days to watch the girls go by—the attraction being what the wind did to the ladies' skirts. The New York police were called to disperse this group of oglers with such regularity that the routine came to be known as the "23 skiddoo." From this beginning, the expression "23 skiddoo" came to mean "beat it."

Ever Wonder Why?

—old shoes are tied to the bumper of a bride and groom's car?

According to ancient custom, shoes were often given as measures of good faith and as an indication of property transferred during business transactions. It is believed that when shoes are tied to the back of the bride and groom's car, they are meant to symbolize the transfer of authority over the bride from her parents to her new husband.

—the Lone Ranger uses silver bullets?

The silver bullets were the idea of Fran Striker, one of the writers who developed the Lone Ranger character for radio. Striker had once written a program about Robin Hood in which Robin Hood dipped the tips of his arrows into melted silver so everyone would know which arrows came from the bow of Robin Hood. This gave Striker the idea of using silver bullets as the Lone Ranger's trademark. The choice of silver made sense, since it had already been decided that the Lone Ranger's means of support would be explained by saying that he had inherited a small silver mine.

—to "put the Kibosh on" something means to put an end to it?

Most probably, this expression comes from two Irish words *cie bais*, which are pronounced "kibosh," and which mean "cap of death." To put the cap of death on something certainly puts an end to it.

Ever Wonder Why?

—when you stare at a red object, then look at something white, you see the image of the object in bright bluish green?

If you have never noticed this effect and would like to see it, draw a red letter "H" about an inch high and stare at the letter's crossbar for 30 seconds. Then, look at a white piece of paper. In a moment, you will see the "H," but it will be bright bluish green.

Why does this happen?

The color white is a mixture of all of the colors in the visible spectrum. If you take one of these constituent colors away from white, you get a different color known as the complement of the color taken away. For example, if you take the color blue away from white, you get yellow, because blue and yellow are complementary colors. And, if you take the color red away from white, you get bluish green, because red and bluish green are complementary colors.

When you stare at something red, such as the red letter "H" mentioned above, the receptors on the back of the eye that detect the color red become tired and soon lose their ability to fully detect that color any longer. If you now look at a white surface, you will see white everywhere, except where the image of the red "H" struck the back of the eye. There you will see white minus the color red, which the eye can no longer detect in that region. That is, you will see the image of the letter "H" in bright bluish green, the complement of red.

Ever Wonder Why?

—that plastic, saucer-shaped sailing toy is called a "Frisbee"?

The inventor of the Frisbee got the idea for the toy from watching college kids toss about tin pie plates used by the Frisbie Bakery Company of Bridgeport, Connecticut. When he developed his plastic version of the pie plate, he decided to call it a "Frisbee," modifying the spelling to avoid legal problems.

—pool tables usually have green playing surfaces?

Pool, or pocket billiards, is believed to have begun as an indoor version of lawn bowling, a game in which heavy wooden balls are rolled across a smooth lawn to position them near a target ball called a jack. Since lawn bowling could not be played in bad weather, a smaller, indoor version of the game was soon invented. The indoor game was played with smaller balls and on a floor mat colored green to simulate the lawn. Before long, it was discovered that the game could be made easier to play by moving the green mat up to a tabletop and by using long sticks to move the balls about. This was the beginning of modern day billiards, a game which is played on a green-top table without pockets and in which the object is to hit and position balls in a manner similar to lawn bowling. Pocket billiards—or pool—came about later when someone decided that it might be fun to knock the balls into holes punched into the tabletop.

So, the tops of pool tables are traditionally green because they were originally designed to look like the green lawns in lawn bowling.

Ever Wonder Why?

—rock singer Gordon Sumner goes by the name "Sting"?

A fellow musician gave the singer this name after seeing him in a yellow and black soccer jersey that brought to mind the colors of a bumblebee. At first, the nickname was "Stinger," but it was later shortened to "Sting."

—cartoonist Bob Kane made his superhero a "Batman"?

When Kane was trying to come up with an idea for his superhero in 1939, he suddenly remembered Leonardo da Vinci's drawing of a bat-winged flying machine that could be attached to a man's body. It was this design of da Vinci's machine that made Kane decide to make his superhero batlike.

The idea for the mask and secret identity, as well as the idea for the Bat Cave, came from the movie *The Mark of Zorro.* The design of Batman's headgear was based on a similar costume worn by a character in another movie, *The Bat Whispers.*

—there are no skycrapers in Washington, D.C.?

As far back as 1791, there have been federal regulations limiting the heights of buildings in the nation's capital so as to protect the panoramic view of the city's monuments. The Building Height Act of 1910 restricted the height of residential buildings to 85 feet and the height of commercial buildings to 130 feet, which are approximately the restrictions that apply today.

Ever Wonder Why?

—a wrench with an adjustable jaw is called a "monkey" wrench?

The wrench is probably named after its inventor, Charles Moncke.

—history contains accounts of the mythical unicorn?

The first written account of the unicorn is provided by Ctesias, the Greek historian who lived in the 4th century B.C. He described an animal he had seen in Persia as being larger than a horse and having a long horn protruding from its forehead. Later, a Roman writer named Pliny described a similar animal and added that it had the feet of an elephant and the tail of a boar.

There seems to be little doubt that the animal both men were describing was a rhinoceros. It is known that rhinoceroses roamed Asia at that time. The animal was called a "unicorn," from two Latin words meaning "one horn."

—the Dead Sea was given that name?

The Dead Sea is an inland sea that lies in a deep fault of the earth's crust. It has no outlets, it is shrinking in size, and it contains so much salt that few plants and no fish can live in it. For these reasons, it was named the "Dead" Sea.

Ever Wonder Why?

—fortune-tellers gaze into a crystal ball?

It is likely that a crystal ball was chosen by the early fortune-tellers because they discovered that gazing at the ball's surface causes the eye to do strange things. When the eye focuses intently on the points of light reflected from any polished surface, the optic nerve gradually tires and becomes unable to send clear images to the brain. The surface begins to appear hazy to the gazer, and in some cases, causes the gazer to go into a hypnotic state. When his happens, the gazer might very well imagine that he or she is seeing into the future.

—witches ride brooms?

According to some accounts, women once used brooms not only for sweeping but also for balance when crossing streams, traveling over rough terrain, and even for vaulting over small obstacles. Because of this image of women and their brooms, it was a natural extension to imagine supernatural witches flying about on broomsticks.

—we say "Don't cross your bridges before you come to them"?

This saying originated at a time when many bridges were so poorly built that travelers often worried about having to cross them. The saying means, don't worry about things—such as rickety bridges—before you have to.

Ever Wonder Why?

—some countries are called "third world" countries?

After World War II, the countries of the world were grouped into three categories: first world countries consisting of the industrialized countries of the Western bloc which have free market economies, second world countries consisting of industrialized countries of the Communist bloc, and third world countries consisting of the poor, underdeveloped countries not aligned with either of the above.

—the legendary vampire had to be killed by driving a wooden stake through its heart?

Not only was the stake to be driven through the vampire's heart, but the deed was to be done while the vampire was lying in his coffin. The purpose of the stake was to nail the vampire to the coffin so he couldn't get out should he be able to revive himself. The requirement that the stake be wooden may have been to symbolize the wooden cross on which Christ died.

—when someone gets caught in his own trap, we say that person was "hoisted on his own petard"?

A petard is a type of bomb once used to knock down walls and gates. To be "hoisted on one's own petard" means to be blown up (hoisted) by one's own bomb. Hence the expression.

Ever Wonder Why?

—a "flea market" is called that?

One of the first, large, open-air markets in this country was the Vallie Market in New York City. When it was found that the full name of the market would not fit on a small street sign giving directions to the market, the name was abbreviated to "Vle. Market." This led people to call it, first the "Vle Market" and then the "Flea Market." Eventually, "Flea Market" became the generic name for this type market.

—wine is kept in colored bottles?

Because direct light causes a chemical reaction in wine that spoils its taste.

—spending time off doing something similar to one's work is called "taking a busman's holiday"?

In the day of the horse-drawn bus, drivers (busmen) sometimes spent their holidays as passengers on their own busses to make sure that their horses weren't mistreated. Time spent in this way soon became known as taking a busman's holiday.

—a light, solid color sports jacket is called a "blazer"?

Students at St. John's College, Cambridge gave the jacket this name because the red jackets worn by the college rowing team were so bright they seemed to be ablaze.

Ever Wonder Why?

—whistling in a theater is considered bad luck?

At one time, stage hands raised and lowered scenery in response to whistled commands from the stage manager. This meant that if someone whistled during a performance, it might very well cause the scenery to move at the wrong time. For this reason, whistling during a performance was taboo, and eventually, whistling at anytime in a theater was considered bad luck.

—a child is often referred to as a "chip off the old block"?

Today, when we hear this expression, we think of the "old block" as a father and the "chip" as his son, but in the very beginning, the "old block" may have actually been an old block!

In the days when pagans worshipped the god Baal and the goddess Astarte, a sacred wooden pole—called the asherah—was erected near altars of worship. It was believed by the worshipers that this pole possessed magical powers, and that if a man could manage to get a chip off of it, the chip would guarantee the fertility of his wife. Therefore, when a son was born to a proud father, it was sometimes thought, "Well, that's a chip off the old block," meaning that the birth was due to the father's having a chip off of the asherah.

Since those days, the chip has come to mean the son himself.

Ever Wonder Why?

—surfers wear those shorts that come down to the knees?

These shorts are called "jams," and they are made as long as they are so that when the surfer is sitting astride the surfboard, his or her thighs won't be chafed as they rub against the edge of the board.

—certain colleges are called "ivy league"?

It has been speculated that the term "Ivy League" derives from the fact that there were originally four (IV) teams in the league (Harvard, Princeton, Yale, and Brown) and that pronunciation of the Roman numeral IV as the letters "I-V" gave rise to the term. However, there seems to be little doubt that when sportswriter Caswell Adams coined the phrase in the mid-1930s, he was simply referring to the ivy that grew on the walls of many of the colleges' older buildings.

—you often see lizards sitting on a light-colored wall?

Lizards use white walls as heaters. Since lizards are cold-blooded animals, they have to rely on the sun for warmth. Since light-colored walls reflect the sun's rays, they are favorite warming places for lizards.

—a divorced or separated woman is sometimes called a "grass widow"?

"Grass widow" originally meant an unmarried mother, supposedly one who would claim to be a widow. The "grass" refers to the bed of grass on which her child was figuratively conceived. The term has since been generalized to mean a divorced or separated woman.

99

Ever Wonder Why?

—so many people type "now is the time for all good men to come to the aid of their party" when trying out a typewriter?

This phrase has no significance other than it contains many of the most commonly used letters of the alphabet. Another phrase often typed is "The quick brown fox jumps over the lazy dog's back." The significance of this phrase is that it uses every letter of the alphabet.

—we decorate our homes with evergreens during Christmas?

In ancient times, it was believed that only by bringing green plants into the home during the winter solstice (December 21 or 22) could one ensure that spring and all of its greenery would return on schedule. So, around the end of December, homes were filled with various types of evergreen plants. After Christ, the same custom was adhered to, and Christians adorned their homes with evergreens around the time of Christmas. After people became reasonably confident that spring would return no matter what they did, the greenery custom continued but was now associated only with the Christmas season.

—the covered wagons of the early west were called "prairie schooners"?

Because when they drove through a field of tall waving grass, their white canvas covers made them look like sailing ships, or schooners, on a sea of green.

Ever Wonder Why?

—many people believe that going swimming right after a meal causes stomach cramps?

This belief is based on the theory that cold water causes a swimmer's blood to rush to the skin to warm it, taking blood away from the digestive organs, thereby causing severe indigestion and stomach cramps. Studies have shown, however, that swimming after a moderate meal produces no such effects.

—when a man shows his affection for a woman, he is said to be "wearing his heart on his sleeve"?

Most likely, this expression originated in the days of chivalry when knights tied their ladies' kerchiefs on their sleeves.

—tortoises are so slow?

Animals have evolved over time with only those capabilities they need for survival of their species. When an animal is fast, it is usually because the animal requires speed to catch its prey or escape its predators. Since a tortoise is a vegetarian, it doesn't require speed to obtain its food. And since, when a tortoise is attacked by a predator it simply withdraws into its hard shell, it doesn't need speed for this purpose either. So, since a tortoise doesn't require speed for its survival, nature hasn't given it any.

It should be mentioned that there are some tortoises whose shells don't offer this kind of protection because they are either soft or too small to retreat into, and in these cases, the tortoises are quite fast on their feet.

Ever Wonder Why?

—VEEP means vice president?

VEEP is simply an abbreviation of VEEPEE for V.P., the abbreviation for vice president.

—a potato is called a "spud"?

"Spud" comes from a Scottish word for a special type of spade that was used to dig potatoes out of the ground.

—people say, "the exception *proves* the rule"?

This is one of our most misused and misunderstood expressions. The word "prove," in this case, is not used in its ordinary sense, but is used to mean "test" as in "*proving* ground." Therefore, what the expression really means is "the exception *tests* the rule." And if, in fact, an exception exists, then the exception *dis*proves the rule.

—at the end of some Jewish weddings, the bridgroom breaks an expensive glass?

This custom goes back to an old superstition which holds that evil spirits sometimes appear at weddings to cast an evil spell on the wedding couple if the spirits become too jealous of the couple's happiness. The breaking of a valuable glass is meant to distract the evil spirits and keep them from bringing bad luck to the marriage.

Ever Wonder Why?

—someone made to take the blame for another's mistake is called a "whipping boy"?

During the Middle Ages, it was considered improper to spank a young prince for his misdeeds. So, as strange as it may sound, the royal family would hire a young companion for the prince and spank him when the prince did wrong. The companion was known as the royal family's "whipping boy," which explains the origin of the term.

—most bricks are red?

The most common type of brick is made from clays that contain the element iron. When the clay is baked during the making of the brick, this iron becomes oxidized, causing the brick to turn red, the color of iron oxide.

—lemon is usually served with fish?

Originally, the lemon was served, not because it gave flavor to the fish, but because it was believed that the acidic juice of the lemon would dissolve any bones that might be swallowed.

Ever Wonder Why?

—the peace symbol is designed as it is?

This symbol, which was introduced by Bertrand Russel in 1958, is based on the letters "N D," standing for Nuclear Disarmament. But, the letters are expressed in semaphore, or flag signals:

Ever Wonder Why?

**—Chic Young's comic strip was named "Blondie"
when it's all about Dagwood?**

When the comic strip was created in 1930, Blondie
wasn't married, and the strip was all about the exploits
of a young single girl named Blondie Boopadoop.
Blondie met and later married a hapless young man
named Dagwood Bumstead.

—a long foot race is called a "marathon"?

In 490 B.C., a young Greek man named Pheidippides
is reported to have run from the village of Marathon to
Athens to carry the news that the Athenians had de-
feated the Persian army in a battle on the plains of Marathon. The distance was 25 miles, and according to the
report, as soon as Pheidippides made his report, he
dropped dead. This story is what led to our calling a
long foot race a "marathon." Today, the length of a
marathon is 26 miles, 385 yards.

**—turkey is the traditional meat served at
Thanksgiving?**

When Governor Bradford initiated the observance of
Thanksgiving in 1621, he sent hunters out to bring back
meat for the celebration. Since wild turkeys were plentiful in New England at that time, it isn't surprising that
most of the meat the hunters brought back was turkey.
From this first celebration arose the custom of serving
that particular meat at Thanksgiving.

Ever Wonder Why?

—we say "Close, but no cigar"?

Cigars used to be awarded to contestants who rung the bell in a carnival game in which one end of a lever is struck with a hammer, sending a sliding weight up a pole toward a bell at the top. If the weight didn't quite reach the bell, the barker might say, "Close, but no cigar."

—flavored ice on a stick is called a "Popsicle"?

Because it is like a lollipop icicle.

—tea merchants began putting tea into little bags?

At one time, samples of tea were given to potential customers in tin containers. One merchant, however—a man named Thomas Sullivan—felt that this was being too generous and decided to put his samples into little silk bags. When people discovered that the bags gave them a convenient way to make a cup of tea without dregs, the bags themselves became in great demand, and thus began the popularity of the tea bag.

—a spiderweb is called a "cobweb"?

"Cob" comes from an old English word "coppe" meaning spider.

Ever Wonder Why?

—the United States is personified by Uncle Sam?

Uncle Sam is based on a real person, Samuel Wilson, a meat inspector from New York. During the War of 1812, Wilson stamped barrels of meat he had approved with the initials "U.S.," standing for United States. But at that time, these initials were not as familiar as they are today, and many people didn't know what they meant. When asked about them, Wilson jokingly said they stood for "Uncle Sam," meaning himself. Thus began the custom of associating the initials U.S. with the name "Uncle Sam," and the idea of a man named Uncle Sam symbolizing the United States.

—we call a horrible place the "Black Hole of Calcutta"?

The Black Hole of Calcutta was an 18 by 14 foot dungeon in a military prison at Fort William in Calcutta, India. It was dimly lit by tiny windows, was as hot as a furnace, and it reeked of sweat and human excrement. In 1756, an Indian ruler overtook Fort William and forced 146 prisoners into this tiny cell. By morning, all but 23 had died. The dungeon had been called the Black Hole even before this, but this horrible event served to strengthen its reputation.

—we stretch?

When parts of the body are not receiving the proper amount of blood circulation, the brain sends out signals causing the body to stretch its muscles. This opens all blood passages and pumps more blood through them, thereby correcting the circulation problem.

Ever Wonder Why?

—when it rains while the sun is shining, it is said that "the devil is beating his wife"?

The explanation behind this saying goes as follows:

Since the sun is shining and there are no clouds overhead to account for the falling water, the water must be something other than rain. At some point in the distant past, it was suggested that the water might actually be tears. And since it was considered unlikely that angels would be crying, it was suggested that the tears were coming from the devil's family, perhaps from his wife while he was beating her.

—when someone rushes about in a violent frenzy, we say that person is "running amuck"?

Amuck, or Amoq, is the name given to an extraordinary form of insanity that occurs only among the people of the Malay Peninsula. When the disorder strikes, the victim grabs a weapon and runs wildly through the streets killing until he is killed. When it is recognized that someone is having one of these fits, a cry of "Amoq! Amoq!" is sent out to warn others. This is where we get the expression, "running amuck."

—a vodka and tomato juice cocktail is called a "Bloody Mary"?

The cocktail was named after another Bloody Mary, Queen Mary I of England, who is known for her vengeful and bloody treatment of Protestants.

Ever Wonder Why?

—we toss confetti during festivities?

"Confetti" is from the Italian, meaning candy, and at one time, confetti was, in fact, candy in the form of bonbons tossed from balconies at carnival time. Later, smaller—and less expensive—hard candy was substituted, and this form of confetti had to be wrapped in paper to prevent it from hurting the people below. Eventually, the candy itself was omitted, and just the paper was thrown. The paper alone was then called "confetti."

—Christmas songs are called "carols"?

The word "carol" comes from a Middle English word *carolen*, meaning "to sing joyously."

—wakes are held for the recently deceased?

Evil spirits, it was once believed, rushed to the scene of a recent death to lure the dead person's soul to hell. But these spirits, according to belief at that time, would be afraid to approach the body of the deceased in the presence of bright light and human activity. Therefore, to protect the soul during its brief passing from earth to heaven, all-night vigils, called wakes, were held by the deceased's family and friends. The term "wake" comes from an old English word meaning "to be active."

Ever Wonder Why?

—some people believe that washing one's car will make it rain?

The idea behind this superstition is the same as that which prompts the Indian rainmaker to pour water on the ground during his incantation. The idea is that, by imitating a desired event on a small scale, one can cause the event to occur on a larger scale. Thus, when someone pours water on his car, the gods assume he is asking for a downpour—and they usually give it to him.

—a slide fastener on clothing is called a "zipper"?

Like so many things, the zipper got its name through a misunderstanding. In the early 1920s, the B.F. Goodrich company used this type of fastener on a new line of rain boots called "Zipper Boots." When the boots were introduced, the public thought the term "zipper" applied to the boot's new type of fastener, and from that day, the fastener has been called a "zipper."

—at Christmas we decorate with wreaths of holly?

It has been suggested that the holly wreath is symbolic of the crown of thorns worn by Christ.

Ever Wonder Why?

—mistletoe grows in the tops of trees?

Mistletoe is a parasitic plant that feeds off of the trees on which it grows. Where it takes root on the tree is determined primarily by birds that feed on the plant's berries.

The white berries of the mistletoe plant contain tiny seeds covered with a sticky substance called viscin, and when fruit-eating birds eat the berries, some of the seeds stick to the birds' beaks. Later, when the birds clean their beaks by scraping them against the branches of other trees, the seeds stick to the branches, take root, and the plant begins to grow. Since birds usually perch—and clean their beaks—on the upper branches of trees, that is where mistletoe is usually found.

A second determining factor is sunlight. Mistletoe requires a great amount of sunlight to flourish and, therefore, grows best on the upper branches of trees where sunlight is plentiful.

—some Hindu women wear a red dot on their forehead?

The red dot is called a *tilaka*—or sometimes, a *tika*—and it indicates that the woman is married.

—the Dutch wear wooden shoes?

Dutch farmers who worked in fields of mud and standing water discovered long ago that shoes made of wood don't deteriorate under wet conditions as would leather shoes. The wooden shoes were also found to be easier to clean and easier to step into and out of when leaving or entering a building.

Ever Wonder Why?

—salt preserves meat?

Salt combines with the moisture in the meat to form a saline solution so strong that it restricts the growth of certain types of harmful microorganisms.

—the day celebrating the resurrection of Christ is called "Easter"?

"Easter" comes from an old English word "Eastre." Eastre was the name of a pagan goddess of spring and also the name of a spring festival held in her honor in April. At one time, April was known as Easter-month. When the Christians began celebrating the resurrection of Christ at about that same time, the celebration itself was called "Easter."

—when you see a statue of a general on his horse, the horse is sometimes rearing up, sometimes walking, and sometimes standing still?

According to an old principle—one which has not always been followed—the position of the horse's feet tell you how the general died. If all four feet are on the ground, he died of natural causes; if one foot is raised, he died of wounds sustained in battle; and if two feet are raised, he died on the field of battle.

Ever Wonder Why?

—there is a nursery rhyme about London Bridge falling down?

"London Bridge is Falling Down" is a very old song that was inspired by the fact that, for many years, the original London Bridge did show signs of falling down, as in 1437, for instance, when its tower and three of its arches collapsed. But the song may go back further than that to 1282 when large chunks of ice in the Thames river knocked down several of the bridge's arches. The bridge was finally rebuilt and made safer in 1831.

—scoring three goals in a hockey game is called a "hat trick"?

One definition of "trick" is the process of doing a thing successfully, and a "hat trick" has come to mean the process of doing three things successfully. It originated in the game of cricket where, at one time, if a player scored three consecutive wickets, he was awarded a hat.

—criminals were once executed at sunrise?

At the time this practice arose, it was policy to carry out executions as soon as possible on the day set by the court. However, the execution had to wait until sunrise on that day so the firing squad could see their target.

Ever Wonder Why?

—it was once believed that crickets in the home bring good luck?

When crickets find their way into a house, they usually stay near a fireplace because they enjoy the warmth. Long ago, when people believed in the presence of spirits more than they do today, this led some to put forth the theory that crickets are actually the spirits of old people recently deceased. This being the case, it was believed that crickets should not be harmed or bothered in any way, and that if a cricket chose to leave a person's house, it was a sign of bad luck for that person. Conversely, if the cricket chose to remain, it was a sign of good luck.

—most of us are right-handed?

It may be that we are right-handed because primitive man believed his heart was on his left side. According to one theory, man learned very early that his heart was his most vital organ and one to be protected at all times. Since early man felt his heartbeat under his left breast, he assumed that the heart was located there. So, when he fought—as he did constantly—he instinctively kept his left side back and his right side forward. This made it necessary for him to do his fighting and wield his weapon with his right hand, keeping his left hand in a position to protect the heart and fend off blows to that region of the body. According to the theory, this eventually led to the right hand responding to signals from the brain with greater efficiency than the left hand, and this is what eventually led to right-hand dominance.

Ever Wonder Why?

—black armbands are worn to express mourning?
Black armbands were adopted in England years ago as a way to dress servants for mourning rather than outfitting them in full black uniforms.

—we say "It ain't over till the fat lady sings"?
Not long ago, when the Philadelphia Flyers hockey team played a home game, the evening was always concluded with a rather large female vocalist singing "America the Beautiful." If a game neared its end with the Flyers behind in the scoring, the fans were sometimes told not to give up hope because the game "ain't over till the fat lady sings." Thus goes one explanation of the origin of this expression.

—high school sweaters have one or more rings on the upper right arm?
The rings have no significance now, but originally, they indicated the number of years a student had been a member of a sports team.

—brides wear veils?
Originally, only virgin brides wore veils, and the purpose of the veil was to conceal the bride's blushes. After the original purpose was forgotten, the veil remained a part of the bride's trousseau.

Ever Wonder Why?

—there were once brass rings on merry-go-rounds?

The merry-go-round, or carousel, grew out of a game devised eight hundred years ago in Arabia to train horsemen for battle. The Spanish crusaders introduced the game to Europe and called it "carosella," which means "little war." Later, the French modified the game—which they called "carousel"—and added an event in which the horsemen attempted to spear small rings suspended on ribbons between two posts. In 1680, someone in France got the idea of building a mechanical version of the game to train the young nobility in the art of ring spearing. The mechanical device consisted of wooden horses and chariots attached to a rotating center that was turned either by a horse or by several men. Mounted to one side were one or more small rings which the young riders were to try to spear with their small lances.

Later, when the carousel became a device ridden for amusement, the ring was made of brass and the object was simply to grab it for a free ride. It wasn't until the 18th century that the ride was called a "merry-go-round."

Ever Wonder Why?

—those World War I airplanes with machine guns on the fuselage didn't shoot their propellers off?

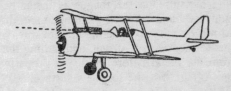

For a long time this presented a problem. But in 1915, a Dutch designer named Anthony Fokker devised a method for synchronizing the propeller with the machine gun so that the gun stops firing whenever a propeller blade is directly in front of it.

—Scottish names often begin with "Mac"?

"Mac" simply means "son of." Therefore MacMahon means son of Mahon, the latter usually being the name of the ancestor who started the clan.

The Irish counterpart of "Mac" is "O," as in O'Brien, which means son of Brien.

—rum diluted with water is called "grog"?

Admiral Edward Vernon of the British West Indies fleet was nicknamed "Old Grog" because he was fond of wearing a large coarse coat made of grogram. In 1740, Vernon decided that all sailors aboard ships should be given a daily ration of rum mixed with water because, according to some accounts, he believed the drink would help prevent scurvy. In honor of "Old Grog," the sailors began referring to diluted rum as "grog."

Ever Wonder Why?

—your tongue sticks to cold metal?

When a moist tongue touches a piece of very cold metal, the moisture on the tongue is instantly frozen, creating an ice bond between the tongue and the metal. It would not be wise to experiment with this, since the bond thus formed is very strong, and pulling the tongue away from the metal before the ice is properly melted could tear off part of the tongue's surface.

—it was once considered bad manners to put one's elbows on the table at mealtime?

This rule of etiquette came about at a time when tables were usually so crowded that there simply wasn't room to prop one's elbows on the table without crowding another diner. With tables less crowded today, putting one's elbows on the table is no longer considered bad manners.

—the upper canine teeth are called "eyeteeth"?

Because the roots of these teeth extend upward almost to the eyes.

Notes

Page	Why	Principal Source(s)
3	—the scale in music is sung, "do re mi fa so la ti do"?	*The International Cyclopedia of Music and Musicians* by Oscar Thompson (New York: Dodd Mead, 1985), 883.
		Encyclopedia of Word and Phrase Origins by Robert Hendrickson (Facts on File Publications Network, 1987), 168.
		Grove's Dictionary of Music and Musicians 5th Ed. by Eric Blom (New York: St. Martin's Press, 1955), 7:880–881.
8	—most roadside mailboxes are the exact same size, shape, and design?	*R.F.D. Country!* by Bill and Sarah Thornbrook (West Chester, PA: Schiffer Publishing, 1988), 13.
14	—a whip cracks?	*Understanding Physics: Volume I* by Isaac Asimov (New York: Walker & Company, 1966), 166.
		Conceptual Physics: 4th Ed. by Paul G. Hewitt (Boston: Little, Brown & Company, 1981), 295.

20	—listening in on another person's conversation is called "eavesdropping"?	*An Etymological Dictionary of the English Language* by Rev. Walter W. Skeat (Oxford: Clarendon Press, 1961), 187–188.
		Dictionary of Word and Phrase Origins by William and Mary Morris (New York: Harper & Row, 1977), 198.
23	—Christmas is sometimes written "Xmas"?	*The Random House Dictionary of the English Language (2nd Ed.)* (1987), 2196.
24	—we say "sic 'em!" to a dog?	*Webster's New World Dictionary*
		Random House Dictionary of the English Language 2nd Edition, (1987).
		Webster's Third New International Dictionary 1971
25	—there is no "Q" or "Z" on a phone dial?	Harrison McClauren, Southern Bell
24	—the "BRIDGE ICES BEFORE ROAD"?	*Science in the World Around Us* by William Charles Vergaro (New York: Harper & Row, 1973), 144.
32	—pretzels are made in that loose-knot pattern?	*Why Did They Name It?* by Hannah Campbell (New York: Fleet Publishing, 1964), 23.
		World Book Encyclopedia (1989), 7:329.
33	—a moth will circle a light at night?	*Random House Book of 1001 Questions and Answers About Animals* by Michele Staple & Linda Gamlin (New York: Random House, 1990), 25.

34	—hair growing in front of the ears is referred to as "sideburns"?	*Dictionary of Misinformation* by Tom Burnam (New York: Crowell, 1975), 229.
		A Dictionary of Slang and Unconventional English by Eric Partridge (New York: MacMillan), 1068.
		Encyclopedia Britannica, 3:328.
45	—actors are wished good luck by telling them to "break a leg"?	*Bodywatching* by Desmond Morris (New York: Crown, 1985), 59.
47	—very hot summer days are called "dog days"?	*Curiosities of Popular Customs* by William S. Walsh (Philadelphia: J. B. Lippincott, 1925), 339.
		Oxford English Dictionary (2nd Edition) Volume 4.
47	—June is such a popular month for weddings?	*Curious Customs* by Tad Tuleja (New York: Harmony Books, 1987), 52.
50	—an oboe is usually the first instrument you hear when an orchestra warms up?	*Inside Music* by J. Raymond Tabin (New York: Emerson Books, 1969), 14.
64	—attempted deception referred to as "mumbo jumbo"	*Travels of Mungo Park* by Ronald Miller, ed. (New York: E.P. Dutton, 1954), 29
66	—the moon looks larger when it is near the horizon?	*Visual Illusions* by M. Luckiesh (New York: Dover Publications, 1965), 169.
		ABC's of Nature by Richard Scheffel, ed. (Pleasantville, New York: Reader's Digest Association, 1984), 12.

68	—there is always a wad of cotton in new bottles of pills?	Wayne Buff, College of Pharmacy, University of South Carolina.
70	—a chess player says "checkmate" when he captures his opponent's king?	*The Past of Pastimes* by Vernon Bartlett (Archon Books, 1969), 84.
		Encyclopedia Britannica (1972), 5:457.
85	—golf balls have dimples?	*The Flying Circus of Physics* by Jearl Walker (New York: John Wiley & Sons, 1977), 102, 262.
87	—you see blue sparks when you chew a wintergreen mint in a dark room?	*Encyclopedia of Physical Science and Technology 2nd Ed.* by Robert A. Meyers, ed. (New York: Academic Press, 1992), 9:179.
89	—"23 skiddoo" means "beat it"?	*Morris Dictionary of Word and Phrase Origins 2nd Edition* by William and Mary Morris (New York, Harper & Row, 1962), 586.
90	—old shoes are tied to the bumper of a bride and groom's car?	*Wedding Toasts and Traditions* by Mark Ishee (J. M. Productions, 1986), 35.
97	—a "flea market" is called that?	*Encyclopedia of Word and Phrase Origins* by Robert Hendrickson (New York: Facts on File Publications, 1987), 199.
101	—when a man shows his affection for a woman, he is said to be "wearing his heart on his sleeve"?	*Why Do We Say It* (Secaucus, New Jersey: Castle, 1985).

106	—a spiderweb is called a "cobweb"?	*Barnhart Dictionary of Etymology* by Robert K. Barnhart, ed. (H. W. Wilson, 1988), 184.
		Morris Dictionary of Word and Phrase Origins 2nd Edition by William and Mary Morris (New York: Harper & Row, 1962), 138.
108	—when someone rushes about in a violent frenzy, we say that person is "running amuck"?	*Curiosities of Popular Customs* by William S. Walsh (Gale Research, 1966), 39.
110	—a slide fastener on clothing is called a "zipper"?	*Stories Behind Everyday Things* by Jane Polley, ed. (Pleasantville, New Jersey: Reader's Digest Association, 1980), 400.
112	—the day celebrating the resurrection of Christ is called "Easter"?	*Easter and Its Customs* by Christina Hole (New York: M. Barrows and Company, 1961), 11.
		World Book (1989), 6:37.
		Concise Oxford Dictionary of English Etymology by T. F. Hoad, ed. (Oxford: Clarendon Press, 1986).
113	—criminals were once executed at sunrise?	*Answers to Questions* by Frederic J. Haskin (Washington, DC: Frederic J. Haskin, 1926), 134.
		Why Do Some Shoes Squeak by George W. Stimpson (New York: Bell Publishing, 1984), 119.

Index

128

129